DATE DUE

JUL 28 1997		
FEB 6 1998		
MAY 1 4 2005		

D1071572

Mary Tyler Moore

GREAT ACHIEVERS:

LIVES OF THE PHYSICALLY CHALLENGED

Mary Tyler Moore

Margaret L. Finn

Chelsea House Publishers

Philadelphia

CHELSEA HOUSE PUBLISHERS

EDITORIAL DIRECTOR Richard Rennert
EXECUTIVE MANAGING EDITOR Karyn Gullen Browne
COPY CHIEF Robin James
PICTURE EDITOR Adrian G. Allen
PRODUCTION MANAGER Pamela Loos

Staff for MARY TYLER MOORE
SENIOR EDITOR Kathy Kuhtz Campbell
ASSOCIATE EDITOR Therese DeAngelis
EDITORIAL ASSISTANT Kristine Brennan
DESIGNER Cambraia Magalhaes
PICTURE RESEARCHER Patricia Burns
COVER ILLUSTRATOR Daniel O'Leary

First Printing

1 3 5 7 9 8 6 4 2

Library of Congress Cataloging-in-Publication Data

Finn, Margaret L.
Mary Tyler Moore, actress / Margaret L. Finn.
p. cm. — (Great achievers)
Includes bibliographical references and index.
Summary: Examines the personal and professional life of the popular television actress.
ISBN 0-7910-2416-4   0-7910-2417-2 (pbk.)
1. Moore, Mary Tyler, 1937 —Juvenile literature. 2. Entertainers—United States—
Biography—Juvenile literature. [1. Moore, Mary Tyler, 1937-   . 2. Actors and
actresses. 3. Women—Biography.] I. Title. II. Series: Great achievers (Chelsea
House Publishers)
PN2287.M697F56 1996   95-37555
791.45'028'092—dc20   CIP
[B]   AC

FRONTISPIECE:
Actress Mary Tyler Moore arrives at the Emmy Awards ceremony in
Pasadena, California, on September 20, 1987. As of 1996, Moore has
received seven Emmys for various television performances over the
years.

CONTENTS

GREAT ACHIEVERS:

LIVES OF THE PHYSICALLY CHALLENGED

JIM ABBOTT
baseball star

LUDWIG VAN BEETHOVEN
composer

LOUIS BRAILLE
inventor

CHRIS BURKE
actor

ROY CAMPANELLA
baseball star

RAY CHARLES
musician

BOB DOLE
politician

STEPHEN HAWKING
physicist

ERNEST HEMINGWAY
writer

JACKIE JOYNER-KERSEE
champion athlete

HELEN KELLER
humanitarian

RON KOVIC
antiwar activist

MARIO LEMIEUX
ice hockey star

MARLEE MATLIN
actress

MARY TYLER MOORE
actress

FLANNERY O'CONNOR
author

ITZHAK PERLMAN
violinist

FRANKLIN D. ROOSEVELT
U.S. president

HENRI DE TOULOUSE-LAUTREC
artist

VINCENT VAN GOGH
artist

STEVIE WONDER
musician

A MESSAGE FOR EVERYONE

Jerry Lewis

Just 44 years ago—when I was the ripe old age of 23—an incredible stroke of fate rocketed me to overnight stardom as an entertainer. After the initial shock wore off, I began to have a very strong feeling that, in return for all life had given me, I must find a way of giving something back. At just that moment, a deeply moving experience in my personal life persuaded me to take up the leadership of a fledgling battle to defeat a then little-known group of diseases called muscular dystrophy, as well as other related neuromuscular diseases—all of which are disabling and, in the worst cases, cut life short.

In 1950, when the Muscular Dystrophy Association (MDA)—of which I am national chairman—was established, physical disability was looked on as a matter of shame. Franklin Roosevelt, who guided America through World War II from a wheelchair, and Harold Russell, the World War II hero who lost both hands in battle, then became an Academy Award–winning movie star and chairman of the President's Committee on Employment of the Handicapped, were the exceptions. One of the reasons that muscular dystrophy and related diseases were so little known was that people who had been disabled by them were hidden at home, away from the pity and discomfort with which they were generally regarded by society. As I got to know and began working with people who have disabilities, I quickly learned what a tragic mistake this perception was. And my determination to correct this terrible problem soon became as great as my commitment to see disabling neuromuscular diseases wiped from the face of the earth.

I have long wondered why it never occurs to us, as we experience the knee-jerk inclination to feel sorry for people who are physically disabled, that lives such as those led by President Roosevelt, Harold Russell, and all of the extraordinary people profiled in this Great Achievers series demonstrate unmistakably how wrong we are. Physical disability need not be something that blights life and destroys opportunity for personal fulfillment and accomplishment. On the contrary, as people such as Ray Charles, Stephen Hawking, and Ron Kovic prove, physical disability can be a spur to greatness rather than a condemnation of emptiness.

In fact, if my experience with physically disabled people can be taken as a guide, as far as accomplishment is concerned, they have a slight edge on the rest of us. The unusual challenges they face require finding greater-than-average sources of energy and determination to achieve much of what able-bodied people take for granted. Often, this ultimately translates into a lifetime of superior performance in whatever endeavor people with disabilities choose to pursue.

If you have watched my Labor Day Telethon over the years, you know exactly what I am talking about. Annually, we introduce to tens of millions of Americans people whose accomplishments would distinguish them regardless of their physical conditions—top-ranking executives, physicians, scientists, lawyers, musicians, and artists. The message I hope the audience receives is not that these extraordinary individuals have achieved what they have by overcoming a dreadful disadvantage that the rest of us are lucky not to have to endure. Rather, I hope our viewers reflect on the fact that these outstanding people have been ennobled and strengthened by the tremendous challenges they have faced.

In 1992, MDA, which has grown over the past four decades into one of the world's leading voluntary health agencies, established a personal achievement awards program to demonstrate to the nation that the distinctive qualities of people with disabilities are by no means confined to the famous. What could have been more appropriate or timely in that year of the implementation of the 1990 Americans with Disabilities Act than to take an action that could perhaps finally achieve the alteration of public perception of disability, which MDA had struggled for over four decades to achieve?

On Labor Day, 1992, it was my privilege to introduce to America MDA's inaugural national personal achievement award winner, Steve Mikita, assistant attorney general of the state of Utah. Steve graduated magna cum laude from Duke University as its first wheelchair student in history and was subsequently named the outstanding young lawyer of the year by the Utah Bar Association. After he spoke on the Telethon with an eloquence that caused phones to light up from coast to coast, people asked me where he had been all this time and why they had not known of him before, so deeply impressed were they by him. I answered that he and thousands like him have been here all along. We just have not adequately *noticed* them.

It is my fervent hope that we can eliminate indifference once and for all and make it possible for all of our fellow citizens with disabilities to gain their rightfully high place in our society.

ON FACING CHALLENGES

John Callahan

I was paralyzed for life in 1972, at the age of 21. A friend and I were driving in a Volkswagen on a hot July night, when he smashed the car at full speed into a utility pole. He suffered only minor injuries. But my spinal cord was severed during the crash, leaving me without any feeling from my diaphragm downward. The only muscles I could move were some in my upper body and arms, and I could also extend my fingers. After spending a lot of time in physical therapy, it became possible for me to grasp a pen.

I've always loved to draw. When I was a kid, I made pictures of everything from Daffy Duck (one of my lifelong role models) to caricatures of my teachers and friends. I've always been a people watcher, it seems; and I've always looked at the world in a sort of skewed way. Everything I see just happens to translate immediately into humor. And so, humor has become my way of coping. As the years have gone by, I have developed a tremendous drive to express my humor by drawing cartoons.

The key to cartooning is to put a different spin on the expected, the normal. And that's one reason why many of my cartoons deal with the disabled: amputees, quadriplegics, paraplegics, the blind. The public is not used to seeing them in cartoons.

But there's another reason why my subjects are often disabled men and women. I'm sick and tired of people who presume to speak for the disabled. Call me a cripple, call me a gimp, call me paralyzed for life. Just don't call me something I'm not. I'm not "differently abled," and my cartoons show that disabled people should not be treated any differently than anyone else.

All of the men, women, and children who are profiled in the Great Achievers series share this in common: their various handicaps have not prevented them from accomplishing great things. Their life stories are worth knowing about because they have found the strength and courage to develop their talents and to follow their dreams as fully as they can.

Whether able-bodied or disabled, a person must strive to overcome obstacles. There's nothing greater than to see a person who faces challenges and conquers them, regardless of his or her limitations.

In April 1984, Mary Tyler Moore and her husband, Dr. S. Robert Levine, attend the Academy Awards show in Los Angeles, California. Five months later, Moore, a diabetic, signed herself into the Betty Ford Center for treatment of alcohol-related problems.

1

"LOVE IS ALL AROUND, JUST TAKE IT"

IN SEPTEMBER 1984, a 46-year-old woman sat rigid on a bed at the Betty Ford Center in Rancho Mirage, California, furrowing her brow and biting her fingernail—a portrait of inward desperation. Her face was halved by light and shadow as her inner turmoil marred a pert, large-brown-eyed, short-bouncy-brown-haired prettiness. Around her, brochures were scattered across the bed and table. "Welcome to the Betty Ford Center," one read; another listed the patients' rights and responsibilities: "to keep appointments, avoid unreasonable demands, take part in daily therapy, and abstain from use of alcohol." Baking September sunlight reflected off a stark white building outside and seeped through half-drawn blinds, warming the air-conditioned chill. Mary, known by millions in America as "our Mary," abruptly pulled herself up to her full five-foot seven-inch height at a sound from the door. Slender, statuesque, and grace-ful, she flickered a quick, nervous smile for whomever might be there.

In a startling departure from her public life as television's darling sitcom queen and renowned stage and film actress, Mary Tyler Moore set aside the actor's mask in 1984 and signed herself into the Betty Ford Center for treatment of alcohol-related problems. She went to a place of healing to learn a role she earnestly needed to play.

A friendly staff member appeared in the doorway: she caught herself in a moment of awe upon seeing Moore, then composed her face to a matter-of-fact smile. Ninety-nine percent of the center's clients are not famous, but those who are begin their stay at the center with a blunt no-special-treatment response from the staff. For many celebrities this represents the first time in their adult lives that they can relax, but for others it takes some unpleasant adapting. The center had been founded in 1982 in the affluent Palm Springs suburb of Rancho Mirage as part of the Eisenhower Medical Center by two recovering alcoholics: former first lady Betty Ford and Ambassador Leonard Firestone. By October 1984, approximately 1,000 patients had been treated there with a 75 percent success rate.

"Hello, Ms. Moore?" the staff member said. "I'm here to . . ." Sound and sight faded in and out for Moore, her taut smile wavering. "We need to get you to sign your list of rights and responsibilities . . ." Moore let a six-year-old memory move to the foreground of her mind, recalling a shattering telephone conversation in February 1978 with her husband, television scion Grant Tinker:

> Hello, Mary? It's your sister—she, she's died, Mary. Killed herself . . . it was pills . . . an overdose of . . . Darvon. Oh, God, she'd just broken up with . . . Mary, Elizabeth. Elizabeth is dead.

"And I need to take your sharps, Ms. Moore," the staff member was saying. "It's just hospital policy. Your razor, and any medications you have, and I'm going to have to go through your bag. Just procedure." Moore looked confused and startled. "What? You want my . . . ?" Woodenly, Moore stood back as her privacy was taken away from her, and she

Former first lady Betty Ford greets photographers with a smile as she leaves Long Beach Naval Hospital in May 1978 after being treated for alcoholism and addiction to prescription pain killers. In 1982, Ford and Ambassador Leonard Firestone, also a recovering alcoholic, founded the Betty Ford Center at Eisenhower Medical Center in Rancho Mirage, California, to help treat people with alcohol and drug dependency.

allowed her mind to retrace another conversation from her past, this one from October 1980. Tinker was once again the bearer of bad news:

Mary . . . Richie . . . is dead.

The morning after her admittance to the Betty Ford Center a loud knock at the door startled Moore out of her sleep. "Rise and shine, Ms. Moore! You have bloodwork in fifteen minutes, up by the nurses' station. Rise and shine!" Accustomed to rigorous work schedules, Moore awoke, dressed, and set forth into a peculiar new world filled with

On March 19, 1977, the final
episode of The Mary Tyler
Moore Show is broadcast
on the CBS television network.
In this scene, the WJM-TV
staff console each other after
learning that, with the
exception of anchorman Ted
Baxter (second from right), they
have all been fired by
the new management.

strangers, some groggy, others angry. "What do you mean I
have to do chores?" one woman demanded. "It's part of your
recovery ma'am," a staff person responded in the voice that
first-grade teachers use with recalcitrant students. Dressed in
her usual casual attire—jeans, a work shirt, and sneakers—
Moore sat stiffly, waiting for her blood to be drawn, her arms
folded tight and lines of strain overtaking her attempts at a
cheery smile. That done, she wandered over to the list of
patients' chores on the wall, frowning as she scanned it for
her name.

On another day at the Betty Ford Center, Moore sat in a
circle of patients, most of them wealthy and, like Moore,
dressed casually, unmasked of all pretense. Some tremulous-
ly raised cigarettes to their lips; others restlessly scratched

their arms, no longer anesthetized by gin or vodka, a martini, a beer, cocaine, amphetamines, Valium, Ativan—whatever it took to get them through their days and nights. Dark circles hung like shadows under their eyes, and many rested their sagging heads on propped hands or knees. Others folded their arms tight against their midriffs. Each wore the look of an abandoned child; no one smiled. Withdrawal from drugs and alcohol—most patients at the center were addicted to more than one substance—was characterized by sleepless nights, agitation, feelings of hopelessness, depression, terror, and sometimes attempted suicide. Moore listened to patients "share" some of their inner agony with the group—this was the only support that she would have during her first week at the center. Her new husband, cardiologist S. Robert Levine, who persuaded her to sign into the center after monitoring her blood sugar levels day in and day out, was only allowed to be with her on weekends. For the first time in her life, Moore had to let down her guard and lean on strangers so she could get well.

In these group meetings or alone with a psychiatrist, Moore could let go of the iron control she had displayed to the public and even to friends throughout her acting career. Maintaining her cheerful facade had been difficult, so much so that to ease her tension, she had developed a habit of social drinking at the end of a workday, at dinner, or at a party— nothing unusual, especially in show business with its demanding work schedules, the anxiety of public perfor- mances, and requisite publicity tours. But Moore's life had been complicated by Type I diabetes, which she had been controlling with self-administered insulin shots three to four times per day for 20 years. Her body was unable to produce insulin on its own. Dangerous fluctuations in her blood sugar levels brought on by drinking alcohol had further complicat- ed her life. She had become more fatigued and irritable. And she could not stop drinking on her own.

As another patient shared her stories of the destructive effects of alcohol addiction in her life, Moore's eyes closed for just a moment; she lowered her head and held the weight of it in her hand, looked up to the ceiling, then glanced quickly back and forth to both sides, clasped her hands before her, and grabbed her knee as she slid her sneakered foot on the chair. When she looked up, biting her upper lip, tears flowed easily. Suddenly the taut muscles in her face, her shoulders, and her arms dropped in surrender.

Richie.

Richie had been her only child. Four years earlier, at age 24, he died of a self-inflicted gunshot wound. Richie was gone forever. There was no bringing him back.

Moore raised her hand to share.

According to Betty Ford, "The stigma of drug or alcohol dependency is doubly hard for women because as wives and mothers they are looked upon as people who are the nurturers and caretakers." She added that it is especially difficult for celebrities to "reach inside and come to grips with their situation" because the wall they need to build around themselves is hard to penetrate, and only by doing so do they begin to recover. Dr. John Schwarzlose, director of the center in 1984, said that for famous people, the hardest part of recovery is admitting they have a problem.

On another day, light had returned to Moore's eyes. Drained but more relaxed, she stood with fellow group members—her "family" in the first stages of her recovery from alcohol addiction. Moore's broad smile appeared as she laughed with them, but then a cloud of doubt followed, darkening her face for a moment. Upon hearing about a new activity, she became tense, then relaxed, saying, "Well, OK," and laughingly allowed herself to be blindfolded by a partner. Suddenly it was not funny, though. It was as terrifying as walking blind through a foreign city without being able to speak the language. All of a sudden Moore's dancer timing and grace stiffened into a new, rigid pose: she had to cling to her partner, who would lead her around the center for a full 24 hours. This included walking, climbing stairs, eating, bathing, dressing, even going to the bathroom—all of these activities Moore could do only by trusting another to help her and give her the guidance she would need. Exercises such as this were designed to help people let go of their inflexible, controlling, and overly self-reliant ways; to give them a model for reaching out to others in their everyday lives; and to let friends inside to give support through the blind obstacles of daily life. Patients gradually learn to let others give them what they cannot get enough of on their own—love.

While fumbling in the dark for a day and a night, Moore could not rely on her own judgment. She had to learn to trust. She laughed nervously, then was silent and frightened; but finally easing into a new existence, Moore came closer and hung on, not so coincidentally, to the sensible and open character of Mary Richards. Less than a decade before, she had held on to her colleagues in the final episode of the award-winning *Mary Tyler Moore Show*. Having lost their jobs on the program, the characters all huddled close together, and Mary Richards tearfully reached out to hug them all, smiling and gratefully calling them her "family." In one group hug they maneuvered together to the door, out to the new, uncertain life that they would lead, each building on the love they had for one another. And now, Mary Tyler Moore, blindfolded and willing, reached out, as the theme song of the TV show suggested, to finally take the love that is "all around"—a love that, through her character Mary Richards, she gave for many years to millions of television viewers throughout the world.

Mary performs a dance routine in the early 1960s. Throughout high school she studied dance and took drama and singing lessons, hoping to eventually land an acting job. In 1955, Mary was hired as the Happy Hotpoint elf in a series of television commercials for Hotpoint appliances.

2

TINY DANCER

ON DECEMBER 29, 1937, Mary Moore came into the world, daughter of George Tyler Moore and Marjorie Hackett Moore. She was born into a Catholic family with a proud place in American history: her great-great-great-great uncle John Moore emigrated from England to the United States, arriving in 1765 and later fighting in the Revolutionary War. His son, Captain John Moore, fought in the War of 1812, and his grandson, Lewis Tilghman Moore, fought for the Confederacy in the Civil War.

Mary's father came from a wealthy Virginia family, graduated magna cum laude from Georgetown University in Washington, D.C., and worked as an executive for the Edison Company in New York. Marjorie Hackett's father—Mary's grandfather, Horace Hackett—designed and manufactured the Hackett automobile in the 1920s.

The Moores lived at 491 Ocean Parkway in a small house wedged between two large apartment buildings in a middle-class Irish and Italian neighborhood of Brooklyn, a borough of New York City.

Mary was born at a time when the world stood on the brink of World War II and when the United States was struggling to emerge from the dark days of the Great Depression, when the country experienced widespread business failures, bank closures, and unemployment following the stock market crash of 1929. During this period, American women knew little of the independence that Mary would one day come to represent. Women in the 1930s looked at marriage and child rearing as their only option in life, unless they pursued jobs in nursing or teaching (women in these professions were not expected to marry).

Mary later said of her family, "We weren't poor, but we weren't rich," adding, "I think it gave me a basic preparation for life," creating more motivation in her than a pampered life would have. Her parents chose to send her to a Catholic school, St. Rose of Lima in Brooklyn, where the Sisters of St. Joseph enforced strict military-style school discipline. Each day Mary, wearing her uniform, would file silently into school. During classes she would be expected to sit up straight, with her hands folded on her desk, while she memorized and repeated by rote the questions and answers of the *Baltimore Catechism,* containing the religious teachings of the Roman Catholic church.

But Mary was more rambunctious than academic. She was a tomboy filled with energy, often playing games with the boys. Later Mary spoke of the "battle scars" that she carried with her from humiliation by the nuns. She was made to stand in the boys' row for talking in line after recess, and she was scolded before the whole school yard and kept after school for playing basketball with the boys. Mary then tended to be a loner.

The eldest of the Moore children, Mary would tell reporters many years later that she grew up like an only child. Her youngest sister, Elizabeth, was not born until Mary was 18.

Mary knew at a young age what she wanted and fought hard to get it. At the age of three she wanted a red velvet coat.

"It had to be that or NOTHING," her mother told reporter Frederick Birmingham in 1974. Mary stood posing for a photograph one day, clad in the red velvet coat, with her chin shyly tucked into the Peter Pan collar and one white knee sock sliding down her thin leg to rest in wrinkles just above her ankle and her black Mary Jane shoes. Her round baby cheeks puffed out as she smiled. Mary went on to other declarations: She had had enough of praying to what she thought was herself, so one day instead of saying the Hail Mary (a Catholic prayer to Jesus' mother, Mary), she propped up her rag doll Suzie and firmly intoned, "Hail Suzie, full of grace." But beyond revising one of the most central prayers of the

Residents of Brooklyn, New York, protest the high cost of living during the Great Depression. Mary was born in Brooklyn, four days after Christmas in 1937. The country was still grappling with the economic problems of the depression; however, years later Moore admitted, "We weren't poor, but we weren't rich. . . . I think it [her early childhood in Brooklyn] gave me a basic preparation for life."

*Until she was nine years old,
Mary attended St. Rose of Lima,
a Roman Catholic school,
located on Parkville Avenue
in Brooklyn. Mary, a tomboy,
was frequently scolded by
the nuns for playing with the
boys during recess.*

Catholic church, Mary made up her mind early on about
more personal matters. "From the time I was four years old I
knew what I wanted to be, only then I thought it was a
dancer," she later related to Birmingham. Her mother
recalled that Mary also wanted to act more than anything.
"She was a pain in the neck because she wanted to be a
dancer and an actress so badly," she told reporter Jeff Rovin.

And Mary was "always on a stage, constantly wearing my clothes and putting on a play with dolls for [a make-believe] audience of millions," her mother added. By the age of seven, Mary won her most important battle with her parents: she was able to take ballet lessons.

Mary told reporters that she came from "a happy home," but later she would alter that statement and say that her childhood had been "relatively happy." Her strict Catholic schooling and having to live on and off with an aunt and her proper English grandmother while her parents "weren't communicating" had made life difficult for her. Mary's father also disapproved when she showed little interest in schoolwork, and he "had a hard time demonstrating affection toward me," she recalled. She "craved" that affection, as would any child, and she "bitterly resented" having such "a darn time *getting it,*" she later told Rovin.

When Mary's father landed a job in 1946 as an executive with the Southern California Gas Company, she moved with her parents and her aunt Alberta "Bertie" Hackett, who was a New York NBC radio executive, to Los Angeles. There Mary attended St. Ambrose Grammar School. Her aunt Bertie became business manager of KNXT radio Los Angeles, and her uncle Harold Hackett, who was already living in Los Angeles, was president of Official Films, which produced the television show *Robin Hood.* He had often written to the Moores in Brooklyn telling them of the winter sunshine and his golfing lunches with Bob Hope, urging them to move west.

Bertie Hackett, realizing that her niece was unhappy and lonely in her new neighborhood, decided that Mary had to be the best at something to be accepted by her peers, so she persuaded Mary's mother to enroll her in the neighborhood dancing school. It did not take long for Mary to move to the head of her dance class, and by the time she entered the Immaculate Heart High School, she was also taking drama and singing lessons and giving public performances locally. Mary continued to study dance at the Ward Studio of Dance

Arts while she attended high school, and, as always, she neglected her studies to dance, which led to regular arguments with her parents. Her father "cared nothing for show business," she recalled later. Mary came to resent her parents and longed for independence, rebelling against authority, including her teachers and the Catholic church as well. She thought the church's contention that prolonged kissing was a sin was foolish, and later said, "I think we disagreed on birth control, divorce, and abortion."

At 17, while most girls dreamed of first dates and proms, Mary aspired to something more. Throughout her high school years, clutching letters of recommendation from her uncle Harold, she had approached agents, telling them of her dancing experience. "They wanted to help and were very nice, but they had no way of knowing whether what they were looking at had any ability," she told a reporter for *TV Guide* in 1962. Finally, the day after she graduated from high school in June 1955, Mary tried out for and landed her first job—as the Happy Hotpoint elf, roller-skating around kitchen appliances in a series of television commercials for Hotpoint appliances. Although Mary appeared only three inches high next to a full-sized stove—and her 36-inch bustline had to be painfully bound to a 30-inch one—she earned a whopping $5,000 for her first series of televised ads.

It was as the diminutive Happy Hotpoint elf that Mary came to enlarge her name. There were already five Mary Moores, a clerk told Mary when she went to register with the Actors Equity Association, a union for actors. "Do you have a middle name?" the clerk asked her. "Tyler," Mary answered. "OK," the clerk said. "From now on, you're Mary Tyler Moore." With that decision the clerk made history.

Mary Tyler Moore may have started on the road to stardom, but she remained subject to the rules of her parents because she still lived with them. So in September, three months after her high school graduation, Mary married her next-door neighbor, Richard Meeker, a cranberry juice salesman who was 10 years older than she. Mary later recalled,

"Getting married was the only way I could get out of the house legally since I didn't want to go to college. I obviously didn't know what I wanted when I was 17."

Within two months Mary was pregnant.

In July 1956, at the age of 18, Mary gave birth to Richard Carlton Meeker, Jr. Only three months earlier her mother had given birth to Mary's sister, Elizabeth Moore.

As Mary cared for Richie and took on her domestic chores, she realized that she hated the life of a housewife. "It was sheer drudgery and boredom," she later told Jeff Rovin. "I'd go out of my mind if that's all I had to look forward to." A year after Richie's birth, Mary began to work as a chorus-line dancer on *The Eddie Fisher Show* and *The George Gobel Show*. She landed her first speaking part as Ronnie Burns's

Moore (far right) is seen here around 1958 in a bit part on the television series Steve Canyon, *which dealt with the adventures of an air force pilot, Colonel Canyon, played by actor Dean Fredericks (left). After her marriage to cranberry juice salesman Richard Meeker and the birth of their son, Moore became bored with the life of a housewife and began to work as a chorus-line dancer and bit player in numerous television shows.*

Moore hugs her son, Richard Meeker, Jr., called Richie, who was born in July 1956, when Mary was 18.

girlfriend on *The Burns and Allen Show*, and she went on to garner speaking parts on *The Bob Cummings Show* and *Bachelor Father*.

Mary was still a long way from success as an actress. She had emerged from her rebellious teenage years to intermittent achievements in dancing and acting, but she still had no guarantee of procuring a major part in a television series. Mary could be sure of only two things: her will and her determination to succeed. Little did she know, however, that she would soon land her first television series role as America's most popular "faceless" lady.

Moore poses for a photographer while at an airport in 1962. In 1958, she became popular for her beautiful legs and sexy voice when she played the sultry receptionist Sam on the television series Richard Diamond, Private Detective. *As a gimmick to hook viewers into watching the program, the producers kept Moore's identity a secret and allowed only her legs and hands to be filmed.*

3

"THAT GIRL WITH THE THREE NAMES"

AT AGE 21, hoping to get a regular job in a television series, Moore tried out for and landed her first role—Sam, the sultry receptionist in *Richard Diamond, Private Detective*. As part of a gimmick dreamed up by the producers to "whet the viewer's appetite," they filmed only Moore's long, beautiful legs and her hands as she doodled at her desk and spoke with a sexy voice on the phone, playing mission control for the daring Diamond on assignment. As part of the gimmick, Moore's identity was kept secret from the public and even from the show's star, David Janssen. Making only $80 per week, Moore had been promised more money after 13 weeks with the show, but by that time the producer had been replaced and she did not receive the money. "So I left," she told a *TV Guide* reporter in August 1959. Dick Powell, owner of Four Star Studio, which produced the show, told the story another way. "She got too much publicity and spoiled the gimmick," he said. As Sam, Moore was getting almost as much fan mail as Janssen, and *Variety* magazine had also printed Moore's name four weeks before the show aired.

Despite Moore's popularity as Sam, she was still out of a job. Her friends began to call her "Mary Tyler Maybe." But viewers were eager to see the real Sam, so Moore had little trouble finding other parts in teleplays and different television series, including *77 Sunset Strip*, *The Deputy*, and *Hawaiian Eye*, all popular shows in the 1950s.

In 1959, Moore auditioned for the role of comedian Danny Thomas's daughter on his show *Make Room for Daddy*. With her just-above-the-shoulder hair curled up tightly in a "flip" (a popular hairstyle at the time) and her posture straight, Moore stood tall as she read for the part. Eagerly she glanced over to Thomas, who smiled and looked at her, his long nose dominating his kind face. "Kid," he said, "you're great. You have everything you need for the part. But, frankly, do you think anyone would believe that someone with a nose like mine could have a daughter with a nose like yours?" Moore graciously accepted the rejection and left the studio. But her audition lingered in Thomas's mind.

In the fall of 1961, Moore costarred as Pamela Stewart in her first movie, *X-15,* a semidocumentary about the test launching of the air force's man-guided rocket missile. A *Variety* reviewer wrote that Moore's performance as the wife of one of the three pilots was "competent." He went on to call *X-15* a "good little film" and "surprisingly appealing" with "the most original and tingling shots" being "the gleaming, kaleidoscopic views of the rocket, mirrored in escort cockpits as it hisses higher and higher into the blue." Despite positive critical response, *X-15* was not a box-office success.

The same year that the movie was released, Moore's career took off. In 1960, before the filming of the new comedy series *The Dick Van Dyke Show*, Danny Thomas had remembered Moore. He had said to his partner, the show's creator and writer, Carl Reiner, "How about the kid with the funny nose and those three names?" A call went out to Moore. When she arrived at the studio, "she must have thought I was

Moore is seen here in 1961 on the set of her first movie, X-15, about the testing of a man-guided rocket missile. (She played the wife of one of the air force test pilots.) Although the film received positive reviews from the critics, it was not a box-office hit.

going to kiss her," Reiner reported later. "I got up, I rushed over, I grabbed her, I said: 'Come on—let's *read.*'" They read, and she got the part. With the show's instant success in September 1961, Moore became a star.

For the next five years Moore played Laura Petrie, the perky wife—with her high-pitched, piping voice and compassionate frown—of television comedy writer Rob Petrie, played by comedian Dick Van Dyke. She was mother to a young son, bearing her own son's name, Richie, played by Larry Mathews, and friend to her neighbor, the loquacious Millie, played by Ann Morgan Guilbert. Rose Marie and Morey Amsterdam played Rob's zany fellow writers. Reiner based the half-hour weekly series on his own experiences as a television comedy writer.

At first, Moore played a supportive role to Van Dyke's comic antics. She excelled as, more or less, what is called in comedy a straight man—a comedian's serious partner who presents a contrast to the comedian.

As time went by, Van Dyke spent less time on the set, so entire shows came to be written for Moore by the show's writers (Reiner, Bill Persky, and Sam Denoff), "which she carried off beautifully," according to Reiner. Moore's strength, according to television critics, lay in her timing and her "pert" personality, as well as her "luscious figure" and "wholesome

In a May 1965 episode of The Dick Van Dyke Show, *Rob Petrie (Dick Van Dyke) prepares to take his new motorcycle out for a ride as his wife, Laura (Moore), and their son, Richie (Larry Mathews), look worried. Moore played the perky Laura Petrie from 1961 to 1966, winning the Emmy Award for best actress in 1964 and 1965.*

beauty." Moore brought to the role of Laura Petrie a wide-eyed innocence, a broad smile, a sunny personality, and a determination to personify a dedicated mother and housewife. Although Moore herself hated the life of a housewife, Joanne Stang of the *New York Times* wrote, "Miss Moore has made housewifery a highly palatable pastime. . . . She is neither drudge nor harpy and, while pert, not 'cute' enough to make one gag."

Moore also launched a new fashion trend, wearing slim-fitting Capri pants and flat shoes. "I wanted to portray a house-wife wearing clothing that *I* wore in my kitchen," Moore said. "The sponsors became worried that women might see it as being too avant-garde. Carl Reiner came to my defense and said, 'Women today are not wearing full-skirted frocks with high heels as they vacuum the rug.' " The sponsors agreed to allow Laura Petrie to wear pants in one scene per show. Moore said, "We went along with that for half a season, then we gave them the raspberry [a gesture expressing dislike] and did what we wanted to do." Women all over the country hung up their frumpy housedresses and donned slacks.

According to *Time* magazine, Moore "could beat the pants off any dozen TV actresses" for her acting skill, not just her slacks. Added Stang, "The ladies are grateful to find one of the sorority portrayed with ginger, and they sense—quite accurate-ly—that anyone who seems so nice must really be so."

Moore graduated from appearing almost too young in the early episodes of the series to looking mature, calm, and self-assured in later shows. In the show's first episode, "The Sick Boy and the Sitter," Mary looks like a teenager going to the prom when Laura and Rob attend his boss's party. She stands disapprovingly while Rob plays the clown, her mink stole hanging from her shoulder at an awkward slant, as if she were a child playing dress-up. Her earlier reluctance to leave Richie, who she thinks is sick simply because he refuses a cupcake, detracts from her credibility as an adult and as a mother. However, by episode number 127, "A Farewell to Writing," Mary is stern with Rob, who continually distracts himself from completing his novel. She has changed her hair-style from a flip to a short bouffant with only a hint of that adolescent flipped-up curl in the back. Mary plays the firm mother to Rob's childish whining and procrastinating. But she is not too strict to offer Rob the chance to come home from his friend's cabin "in the mountains," where he has been writing, when his work on his novel has fizzled into solitary paddleball games. Now she is the loving woman, who, if Rob could write, he says, would appear in his book's dedication: "To my darling Laura, who makes life a beautiful thing to write about."

By 1962, *The Dick Van Dyke Show* ranked consistently among the top 15 network programs on television. That year Moore and Richard Meeker divorced, and, according to Reiner, Moore blamed herself for failing to place home before her career. She continued to perform on the show, however, with an award-winning ensemble. In 1963 and 1964 the National Academy of Television Arts and Sciences honored the show with three Emmy awards for outstanding humor, writing, and direction.

As *The Dick Van Dyke Show* prospered, Moore's personal life also took a turn for the better. One day in 1963, a young executive from the Benton and Bowles Advertising Agency, which was connected with the show, came to the set. His name was Grant Tinker. He had graduated from Dartmouth University in 1949, and, unable to find a publishing job when he had first gone to New York, he found a position in management training at NBC. At NBC he worked in radio operations, then left in 1952 to join Radio Free Europe, an organization that broadcast news of the free world to Eastern European countries that, at the time, had no access to uncensored news. Then, with game show host Allen Ludden, he started the long-running hit television quiz show *College Bowl*. In 1954 he directed program development for television at the McCann Erickson Advertising Agency. At that time, advertising agencies, like those representing companies such as General Foods and Johnson's Wax, developed many

television programs. After leaving McCann Erickson, Tinker went on to become vice president of television programming at Benton and Bowles.

Despite Tinker's background and status, Moore paid little attention to him at first. "He was somebody I knew I was supposed to be nice to, and I think that's why I disliked him so much at first," she later told reporter John Bowers. "Also," she said, "I hated him for being so educated and wearing such perfect neckties." When Moore visited New York to promote the show, Tinker surprised her by asking her for a date. Moore said yes, planning to "wow" him on the first date and then turn him down flat when he asked her for a second one. "But it didn't turn out that way," she admitted. Moore spoke of Tinker, who was lean, firm-jawed, and serious, as being "ten-

Moore practices a dance number for her role as the prostitute Holly Golightly in the Broadway musical Breakfast at Tiffany's *in October 1966. The play, which was based on Truman Capote's book of the same name, had several production problems and was canceled after its New York preview.*

Mary Tyler Moore costars with George Peppard in Universal's 1968 film comedy What's So Bad About Feeling Good? *The movie is about a toucan, called Amigo, who carries a "happy virus" into New York, affecting the lives of several people, including Moore's character, a hippie who turns stylish.*

der, exacting, bright, witty and somewhat of a father figure." Within six months—on June 1, 1963—Grant and Moore were married in Los Angeles, and they, Richie, and their three dogs moved into a Beverly Hills mansion that they leased from actor George Montgomery. They spent their weekends at a small seaside apartment.

As Moore delighted in her marriage, she continued to grow in her role as Laura Petrie. Dick Van Dyke and Moore each won Emmy Awards for best acting in a regular television series in 1964 and 1965, and in 1965 she won the Foreign Press Golden Globe Award for best female television personality of the year.

However, Moore soon faced a more personal and permanent tragedy. In 1964, four months into a pregnancy with

Tinker's child, she was rushed to the hospital, where she miscarried. Routine blood work revealed that she was suffering from the most severe form of diabetes: Type I. Blood sugar levels in normal people run from 80 to 120 milligrams per 100 milliliters of blood serum. Moore's registered more than 700 milligrams.

Diabetics are not able to produce their own insulin (a protein pancreatic hormone), which regulates the levels of sugar in the blood. Type I diabetes, formerly called juvenile diabetes because the disease usually appears during childhood or adolescence, occurs when the immune system destroys insulin-producing cells in the pancreas. The cause of the attack continues to elude doctors today. Type I diabetics must inject insulin into their bodies several times each day and limit the amount of sugar and alcohol they consume; Type II diabetics usually do not exhibit symptoms of the disease until they are over the age of 30, and they can control the disease with diet and exercise.

Studies have shown that Type I diabetes may be triggered by a virus, in which case a vaccine may one day be developed to prevent the disease. The studies indicate that the immune system is attracted by a protein on the surface of the insulin-producing cells that comes from a virus infection. Genes and heredity are thought to play a role in Type I diabetes, and researchers have theorized that the virus would bring on the disease only in people whose genes have made them vulnerable to the disease. Some researchers believe that the immune system can even launch an attack on normal cells not infected with a disease organism, a response called autoimmune reaction. It is now generally believed that this is the leading cause of the destruction of pancreatic cells. Any diabetes left untreated can cause deterioration of organs, such as the liver, the kidneys, and the eyes, and can result in coma or death.

At first Moore tried to control her diabetes with diet and exercise, but her sugar levels remained out of control. Afraid to administer the insulin shots herself, she made frequent vis-

Moore and rock and roll legend Elvis Presley (center) take a break with director William Graham during the filming of Change of Habit, *which was released by Universal in 1969. The movie is about a young doctor (Presley) who works in a ghetto and has his opinions changed by a group of nuns, one of whom is played by Moore. Although she had several good acting opportunities in the late 1960s, Moore later said her early movies were so awful that "they're afraid to show them on late night Icelandic TV."*

its to the doctor's office for them. Finally, she found the courage to inject herself. She continued a rigorous regimen of diet and exercise on her own in order to supplement what the insulin shots were doing for her.

Despite her setback, Moore continued to excel as Laura Petrie. Toward the end of the run of *The Dick Van Dyke Show*, it ranked seventh in the ratings. In the show's fifth year, the cast decided to "go out in a blaze of glory" and bring the show to an end. Van Dyke also wanted to pursue a film career. So on March 22, 1966, Moore played Laura Petrie for the last time.

After a summer of rest and relaxation, Moore signed a two-year contract in September with producer David Merrick to play a role that was anything but Laura Petrie—Holly Golightly, a prostitute, in the Broadway musical *Breakfast at Tiffany's*. Scriptwriter and director Abe Burrows based the play on Truman Capote's 1958 novella by that name.

Moore did not have to suffer the hardship of separation from family because Tinker had returned to NBC as head of programming, transferring from the West Coast to the East Coast, and Richie went with her to New York to attend Trinity School, a private school in Manhattan.

Moore rehearsed daily at New York's Mark Hellinger Theater on 51st Street. She arrived one day wearing a scarf over her head, a checkered coat, and white shiny boots. Before entering the theater she put a cigarette into a holder and lit it. A reporter asked if she was "that pretty, rather uncomplicated girl who had been waltzing into Dick Van Dyke's living room all these years in a welter of apple-pie wholesomeness." "I'm the sweaty-palms girl," she answered. "I'm just so terrified I'm going to be bad in front of a lot of people. I just have to be good." She then marched into the rehearsal with a look of fierce, if not frightened, determination. Onstage, Moore transformed herself into the young Holly, who collected $50 from her many dates as "powder room change."

Capote, dressed in a blue suit, peered intently through spectacles at Moore from his seat in the orchestra. When reporter Jeff Bowers asked him if Mary Tyler Moore was his idea of Holly Golightly, he replied, "Oh, everyone has known a Holly Golightly. One has passed through everyone's life. Now this girl may not be your Holly or mine—but she's possibly someone's," politely withholding his approval of Moore. As he stepped onto the stage to meet Moore and her costar Richard Chamberlain, famed for his portrayal of the handsome Dr. Kildare in the television series of the same name, Moore squirmed like a child, holding her arms behind her. She admitted later, "It was the worst moment being on stage while Capote was down front. I didn't want to be bad!"

Moore was not "bad," but a severe case of laryngitis hampered her singing in the preview show in Philadelphia the following Wednesday, and she was so afraid before the performance that she admitted to writer Bowers over a steak dinner in a kosher restaurant across from the Forrest Theater that her knees actually shook onstage. "I have a nightmare that I've had practically all my life," she said. "I'm on a beach and these huge tidal waves come in. I fight, but they carry me away. I claw at the sand, and yet they take me away. I don't know why I dream it. I love the sea." When asked why she put herself through so much anxiety, she responded, "Because I have to be the greatest. I'm not doing this for anybody on earth except for myself. It's something deep inside me that has to be expressed." After the interview, Moore pulled a scarf over her head and ran in sneakers across the alley to the stage door, where teenagers waiting for her autograph failed to recognize her. That night Moore, in her dark glasses, stepped onstage to resounding applause for her first stage appearance. According to Bowers, despite her laryngitis, "with some kind of inner strength that is denied most of us, [Moore] forced a voice that was cracked . . . to go brightly through songs."

Capote, after watching the performance in Philadelphia, predicted a 14-month run of "a successful but not a distinguished musical." *Breakfast at Tiffany's* would not fare so well in New York, however. Merrick fired Burrows and hired Edward Albee, who changed Chamberlain's character into "that ghastliest of theatrical waxworks," according to *Newsweek* critic Mel Gussow, "The Author Chatting with His Characters." Critics attacked Albee, and in the end Merrick, "bored" with the production, canceled it after its New York preview performance, losing his $500,000 investment and damaging Moore's reputation as an actress. The fault seemed not to lie with Moore, however, but with the production itself. Moore rebounded from the failure of her Broadway venture. She went on to sign a six-picture contract with Universal Pictures that brought more flops than hits. In 1967 she costarred with actress and singer Julie Andrews, acclaimed for her stage performances in *Camelot, My Fair Lady,* and *The Sound of Music.* Moore played the prim and proper roommate to Julie Andrews's character in *Thoroughly Modern Millie.* Although Andrews's performance netted her subsequent outstanding film roles, Moore's "unappealing role," according to *Newsweek* reporter Paul Zimmerman, gave her little room to excel. Then, in 1968, Moore was miscast as a hippie who turns chic when a tropical bird infects New York City with a euphoria-spreading virus in *What's So Bad About Feeling Good?* The following year, she played a nun opposite rock and roll star Elvis Presley as an urban ghetto doctor in *Change of Habit* and received tepid reviews. Moore later said that her early movies were "so bad they're afraid to show them on late night Icelandic TV."

After all of Moore's disasters since her last performance on *The Dick Van Dyke Show*, things could not have looked more grim. "Though only 32, Moore seemed to have reached a professional dead end," James Stewart-Gordon wrote for *Reader's Digest.* She wanted to return to television, but the industry now found it all too easy to believe that she was not really talented but had merely ridden to her Emmys on the coattails of Dick Van Dyke. At a time when the sky loomed darkest over the career of "that girl with the three names," an unexpected phone call came that would change the course of her career—and her life.

Moore and husband Grant Tinker outside the 1965 Emmy Awards ceremony.

4

"MAKING IT AFTER ALL"

"OUT OF THE BLUE," as Muriel Davidson of *Good Housekeeping* wrote in 1969, CBS offered Dick Van Dyke a one-hour variety special. Van Dyke, needing a focus for the show, turned to Mary Tyler Moore, his television wife of the halcyon Rob and Laura Petrie days.

The nostalgia special, "How to Succeed in the 70s Without Really Trying," combining the comedy, dance, and singing talent of both stars, aired on April 13, 1969, and drew one of the highest ratings ever recorded. "Mary was gangbusters in that special," Grant Tinker said. "I don't think Dick threw it to her, but he certainly gave her plenty of funny things to do." The CBS that had forgotten about the woman who played Laura Petrie now seemed to realize it had discovered a star. CBS and the other two major television networks of the time, ABC and NBC, offered Moore her own show, but CBS told her that no matter what idea she came up with, it would be called *The Mary Tyler Moore Show*.

Moore and Tinker accepted the CBS offer on the condition that they would get a series commitment, and CBS responded with a 13-episode contract. The husband-and-wife team then started their own production company, MTM Enterprises, with Moore as chairman of the board. She had wanted to name it GAT, Tinker's initials, because she knew that he would run the company, but he felt that she had earned the commitment, so she deserved the credit and the name.

But before *The Mary Tyler Moore Show* could fly, it would have to chip away at a very tough shell—and avoid getting squelched altogether. Jim Brooks and Allan Burns had a fair amount of experience in the television industry, but their ideas for the show ignited a controversy that nearly ended the program before it had started.

Brooks had been a writer for CBS News in New York and a writer and producer of documentaries. Burns had been the writer and creator of *The Munsters*, a writer for *The Smothers Brothers Show*, and an editor of *Get Smart.* The men had previously worked together in 1969 and 1970 on the widely respected television series *Room 222*, which centered on the trials and tribulations of a schoolteacher in a large urban public school of diverse population.

Initially they conceived of Moore's character, Mary Richards, as a divorced 30-year-old from Minnesota. Burns recalled, "Mary loved the idea of divorce. It struck her as new territory." Tinker realized, however, that the concept of a series about a single woman living independently in 1970 would be viewed as, "if not revolutionary, a little more *avant-garde* . . . than it would seem today," but he supported it nonetheless. Even though in the show Mary's in-laws would love her and blame their son for the split, Michael Dann, a CBS vice president in Los Angeles, told Brooks and Burns that it would look as if Laura Petrie from *The Dick Van Dyke Show* had divorced Rob. Grudgingly, however, he gave the project verbal approval.

When the two producers flew with Moore's manager, Allan Price, to New York to meet with CBS executives, they met with reluctance to and then all-out rejection of the idea. As they entered a sunless, "womblike" room, Burns reported, a man in the research department presented a list of "forbidden subjects" for television shows: divorce, Jewish people, people from New York, and mustaches. Dann changed his mind and rejected the concept. Later, the CBS executives even told Price to fire Brooks and Burns. Tinker, hearing of this, refused. Because he had told CBS he would not ask them to cover any losses the show might incur, he retained power over the show, but he and the producers knew that angered network officials could kill a show by scheduling it at a time slot during the week when very few people watch television. The divorce concept had to go.

Moore's own divorce from Richard Meeker may have been acceptable to most Americans in 1970, but CBS was reluctant to drive home an image of a divorced Moore to TV viewers every week for some very real historical reasons. Twenty years earlier Ingrid Bergman, a Swedish-born actress beloved to Americans for her roles in *Casablanca, For Whom the Bell Tolls,* and *Gaslight,* left her husband and daughter to have an affair, a child, and eventually a marriage with Italian director Roberto Rossellini. The American press, which had beatified her, suddenly vilified her. On March 14, 1950, Senator Edwin C. Johnson of Colorado called for licensing of actors, producers, and films to keep immorality out of the country, adding that Bergman had perpetrated "an assault upon the institution of marriage." He went on to call Bergman "one of the most powerful women on earth today . . . and a powerful influence for evil." Finally, he said, "Under our law no alien [meaning both Bergman and Rossellini] guilty of turpitude [a vile act] can set foot upon American soil again." Johnson did conclude that Bergman may not have "destroyed her career for naught," adding, "Out of her ashes may come a better Hollywood."

Bergman's career did not end; rather, it flourished, although it was a long time before she returned to the United States. Her scandal may have caused CBS executives to envision *The Mary Tyler Moore Show* in ashes after its first flight, especially because Johnson's description of Bergman as a "sweet and understanding person with an attractive personality which captivated everybody on and off the screen" could have equally described Mary Tyler Moore, her character of Laura Petrie, and the Mary Richards she was to portray in *The Mary Tyler Moore Show*.

Brooks and Burns were angry, however. They wanted to quit, but with a week remaining to create a new concept, they stayed with the show. "Somehow we thought [quitting] would be very damaging to Mary and Grant," Burns said, so they stayed "because Mary and Grant had been so good and decent to us, so supportive since [the project] started."

By January 10, 1970, the basic show concept, the characters, and the physical layout were ready: Mary Richards would still be single, 30 years old, and a Minnesota native, but now she would be building a new life after a failed romance. No divorce. Yet although MTM Productions had its first situation comedy (sitcom) format, it still had only two employees (Brooks and Burns), an empty office, one actress, and just eight months to cast the characters, write the script, rehearse, and produce the opening show.

At the same time, although perhaps not consciously, Brooks, Burns, Tinker, and Moore found themselves at the threshold of a brand-new era in television comedy. The original television situation comedy in America, peopled by characters that became as familiar to the audience as friends and family, had provided a sense of "family warmth without confusion, without ambiguity," and the characters themselves were members of an actual family, according to Jeff Greenfield, author of *Television: The First Fifty Years*. Sitcoms, along with other comic shows featuring sight gags, slapstick humor, and stand-up comics, emerged as a transplant from radio, Michael Winship wrote in *Television*. There were programs like *The Burns and Allen Show* (1950–58), featuring the comic husband-and-wife team, and *The Jack Benny Show* (1950–65), on which Benny told jokes in between

strains on his violin. Also running at this time was *The Honeymooners*, featuring Jackie Gleason as the fat, loud-mouthed, blue-collar husband (and model for the animated series character Fred Flintstone), with wife and buddy in tow. Perhaps the most prominent show of this genre was *I Love Lucy*, with comedian Lucille Ball and her husband Desi Arnaz, featuring comedy so oddball and heartwarming that the show continues to air today in reruns throughout the world.

These feel-good shows came of age in the 1950s, during the post–World War II "era of prosperity and alleged [happiness]," Winship wrote. He noted that the 1950s were not exactly such simple times: with the House Un-American Activities Committee, Senator Joseph McCarthy (chairman of a special Senate subcommittee) drew up "blacklists" of Americans suspected of being Communists. Those listed—many were in the entertainment industry—often could no longer find jobs, regardless of whether the list was accurate

Lucille Ball and Desi Arnaz in the immensely popular I Love Lucy. *Unlike this and other early TV sitcoms,* The Mary Tyler Moore Show *depicted a woman struggling to succeed on her own.*

Moore (left) as Mary Richards and Valerie Harper as her friend Rhoda Morgenstern on The Mary Tyler Moore Show.

about them. During the 1950s, the cold war between the United States and the Soviet Union also raged silently. "A half hour of visiting the homes of most TV families [then] was like taking a combined dose of Valium and jelly beans," Winship writes. "All was calm; all was sweet." Fathers in these families went off to jobs somewhere and came home, good-naturedly crying, "Hi honey, I'm home" to exuberant children and wives. Other shows in this genre were *Father Knows Best, Ozzie and Harriet,* and *Leave It to Beaver.*

With the Kennedy era in the early 1960s came shows with more "youth and sophistication," according to Winship. Most notable among those was *The Dick Van Dyke Show.* Another show, *Dobie Gillis,* featured a character, Maynard G. Krebs, who was hip and sported the goatee of the Beat generation, or beatniks, the liberal antiestablishment group centered in New York's Greenwich Village. They, in turn, gave rise to the hippies of the 1960s.

But for the rest of the decade, comedy "backslid into silliness" that "made the domestic sitcoms of the 50s seem like high art," Winship writes. With the Vietnam War escalating, television executives must have decided that the American public needed escape, so they rolled out fantasy-based programming. *Bewitched* featured a witch-wife who, with the twitch of her nose, could make anything happen; in *Gilligan's Island* shipwrecked characters blundered about an island paradise week after week. Other sitcoms that followed the same lighthearted idea included *My Favorite Martian*, *The Munsters*, and a show featuring a talking horse, *Mr. Ed.*

"The genre was burned out by the seventies and people were ready for something different," according to Michael Dann. "That something was the truth in comedy, the satire of making fun of bigotry and hate and racial discrimination." These were the sentiments of many Americans at that time—college students, hippies, and average people who marched together to protest the nation's involvement in the Vietnam War, racial discrimination, or the pollution of the environment. Also, the movement for the liberation of women was on the rise across America.

Into this climate of realism and idealism, Brooks, Burns, Tinker, and Moore brought forth their fledgling *Mary Tyler Moore Show*. But they were not alone. They were part of what Winship calls a "three-pronged attack on silly sitcoms." Producer Norman Lear introduced his *All in the Family*, a raw-edged sitcom taking on just about any sensitive topic of the day, from racism to menopause, with the bigoted character Archie Bunker desperately trying to hang onto a world that he could not preserve. *M*A*S*H,* a biting antiwar sitcom featuring Alan Alda as the sardonic Hawkeye Pierce, a surgeon in a field medical unit during the Korean War, just as incisively and hilariously carved away at injustice.

Brooks and Burns assert that they did not intend to address specific political issues. Instead, they attempted to create a very real comedy show, letting stories develop out of the characters themselves. Nevertheless, their Mary Richards was a woman trying to "make it on her own" in a time when single women over the age of 30 were still referred to as spinsters. Moore would change all of that. Her very liberated Mary Richards would become a character as powerful as Senator Johnson thought Bergman was, but in a positive sense, one who could influence the hearts and minds of young girls, women, and men throughout the world. Intentionally or not, Mary Tyler Moore helped shape the consciousness of America during that golden age of television comedy in the 1970s.

But Moore and her producers were still in need of real actors and actresses to play those characters who were to make their dream happen. She codirected casting sessions with the producers and with Ethel Winant, casting director for the show, and, at that time, a vice president at CBS. When Ed Asner read for the part of Mary Richards's boss, the curmudgeonly television news station manager Lou Grant, he disappointed all of them.

Asner, raised in Kansas City, Missouri, attended the University of Chicago and "drifted into theater"; he went to New York City, where he discovered live television. His parts in the renowned prime-time drama shows *Studio One*, *Kraft Television Theater*, and *Armstrong Circle Theater* earned him a costarring role in the 1964 series *Slattery's People*. His performance as a police chief in the made-for-television movie *Doug Selby, D.A.* caught Tinker's eye. He, Brooks, and Burns wanted Asner to read for the Lou Grant character. But drama had hardly prepared him for comedy. After his disastrous reading, the producers told him that it had been intelligent, but they wanted him to come back and read it "wiggly, wild, crazy and far-out."

Instead, Asner told them he would just reread it then, not being sure what they wanted. "Why don't you have me try it now, and if I don't do it right, don't have me back," he suggested. They agreed, and he read it "crazily," he said. They loved it. They told him to just read it that way when he came back to read with Moore. So at that reading he "forced it, pushed it, faked it, and they laughed again," he said. After he left, Moore turned to the others and asked, "Was it that funny?" "There's your Lou," they said, and Asner got the part, despite Moore's initial objections. She had wanted a "nice person" for Lou Grant, just as she had had on *The Dick Van Dyke Show*, Brooks recalled. "That wasn't on our list of priorities."

For the other parts, Moore, Winant, and the producers chose Ted Knight as Ted Baxter, the boorish, addle-brained, and egocentric newscaster; Gavin MacLeod as Murray Slaughter, Mary's office sidekick and WJM-TV's newswriter; and Academy Award–winning Cloris Leachman as Mary's neurotic landlord and friend, Phyllis Lindstrom. But the most important casting after Lou was that of Rhoda Morgenstern, a tough, desperately single Jewish woman from New York, who was Mary's neighbor and soon-to-be best friend. Yet, with a week to 10 days before final shooting of the first episode, *The Mary Tyler Moore Show* still lacked a Rhoda. Actresses that had read for the part seemed too shrill or too angry at Mary during the opening scene of the first episode, which involved conflict between the two characters. Winant feverishly attended plays in the area every night to find the right woman. Finally, she saw a group of sketches at the Melrose Theater in Los Angeles, and there was Valerie Harper. "Oh, my God, she's perfect," Winant recalled thinking. But because Harper was not a member of the Screen Actors Guild (a union of motion picture performers), she was not listed anywhere, and Winant could not locate her. She was just a name in a program with no telephone number or address. Finally Winant's secretary found Harper through a publicity packet sent out to those who attended the play Winant had seen. When it came time for Harper to read for the part, the producers asked her to come dressed down and to wear no makeup. The character they needed was to be *zoftig,* which in Yiddish means "appealingly plump."

Scriptwriter Treva Silverman reports that she was terrified that Harper would be one of those stylishly emaciated actresses and was relieved when Harper walked onstage to read, looking plain and sufficiently overweight.

The interchanges between Rhoda and Mary and between Mary and Lou, rife with conflict, defined the characters and set the tone for the series. Mary meets Rhoda while trying to rent Rhoda's apartment; Cloris Leachman's character, Phyllis, eminently prefers Mary to Rhoda, so she gives Mary a lease, having already promised the apartment to Rhoda. "Get out of my apartment!" Rhoda yells upon seeing Mary in it. Mary fights back, surprising Rhoda and demonstrating Mary's "militant Presbyterian" character. Despite this first go-around, the two are destined to become friends.

Moore and Asner brought to full blossom Mary Richards's defining moment in the first episode: Mary's job interview with Lou Grant. In this scene she demonstrated just how difficult it was for a single woman to enter the male-dominated work world of that time, and Moore reveals brilliantly the range of her comic talent. "Mary was a 'quivering chick,' as the term used then was employed," Brooks said. Dressed in a miniskirt with a bouffant flip hairdo, she sits on the edge of her seat in Lou Grant's office, responding to his gruffly barked questions. Mary furrows her brow, which the producers called "grentioning" to describe her trademark puzzlement, and she displays "her own special brand of inarticulateness and her tendency to sputter in especially tense situations," which they dubbed "fumphering," according to Brooks.

Only Mary Tyler Moore could "grention" and "fumpher" as she did. In the interview scene, Grant first asks if she would like a drink, reaching for a whiskey bottle in his desk drawer. Mary, sitting with ramrod posture, properly declines, but when he insists, she asks for a brandy Alexander—a fancy drink served only in a bar. He replaces the two shot glasses and whiskey bottle in his drawer and quietly suggests coffee. Then he asks Mary about her religion.

 Mary: Mr. Grant, I don't know quite how to say this, but

you're not allowed to ask that when someone is applying for a job. It's against the law.

Lou: Wanna call a cop?

Mary: No.

Lou: Good. Would you think I was violating your civil rights if I asked if you're married?

Mary: Presbyterian.

Lou: Huh?

Mary: Well, I decided I'd answer your religion question.

Wearing her trademark smile, Mary sits at her desk at WJM-TV in an episode from the series' first season.

When Grant asks why Mary is not married, she answers, "55." "Fifty-five reasons why you aren't married?" he barks. "No," she responds. "Fifty-five words per minute."

Pompous WJM anchorman Ted Baxter (played by Ted Knight) strikes a combative pose while Mary tries to play peacemaker. Actor John Amos is at left.

Finally, Mary says, "You've been asking a lot of very personal questions that don't have a thing to do with my qualifications." Silence. Mary looks as though she should not have said that.

> Lou: You know what? You've got spunk.
> Mary: Well . . .
> Lou: I hate spunk.

Mary then accepts the associate producer position that pays $10 less per week than the secretarial job for which she had applied.

The scene, considered by critics to be the "jewel of the show," was to be used in a three-minute promotional shot for the network affiliate stations. But bad lighting and Ed Asner's "too heavy" acting caused Brooks and Burns to scrap the idea.

On February 20, not even out of its egg, the incubating *Mary Tyler Moore Show* was almost smashed by the network, which had slotted its on-air time for Tuesday nights at 8:00 P.M.—the "death slot," according to Allan Burns, because it was opposite the popular *Mod Squad*. Ethel Winant recalled, "What CBS had done was to say, 'You're dead, you're dead as a doornail,' and we knew it." Even though Burns and Brooks had dropped the divorce concept, the network disliked the scripts, thinking they were too unconventional and that the characters were too strange. Additionally, they still disliked Brooks and Burns. But Winant remembered, "Mary was tough. She just wouldn't back down."

To make matters worse, the initial live run-through of the first episode was so fraught with mishaps that it became known as "Black Tuesday." Everything went wrong. The temperature outside was 102 degrees Fahrenheit, and it was so smoggy that Los Angeles had declared a first-stage smog alert. Air-conditioning inside Stage Two in Studio City failed to bring the onstage temperature any lower than the mid-90s, and the cast, crew, technicians, and audience had to wait outside because of a bomb threat in the building. New cameras that would videotape the show simultaneously with the film cameras onto which they had been fitted obscured the stage from the audience. One of the elements that made *The Mary Tyler Moore Show* so special in the long run was that it was performed and filmed before a live audience. Most other sitcoms had been taped with canned laughter dubbed in at the punch lines. But that day, the audience could neither see the actors nor hear them because the sound system was not working. Valerie Harper was too shrill, the man playing Mary's former boyfriend threw down the script in anger, the producers almost lost control and, not being comedians, bombed when they went out to warm up the audience before the show (getting the audience acquainted with the show and in the mood to laugh at its jokes). Burns said, "We were terrified." Brooks added, "It was horrendous." Script supervisor

Marge Mullen reported that the first laugh did not come until the second scene when Lou Grant says, "I hate spunk."

Moore remained calm and, as always, professional. Ethel Winant recalled, "At the end of the show I was so impressed because Mary came out and thanked the audience for hanging in, for staying. I would have been in my dressing room in tears at the end of that awful evening."

But Moore did feel the disappointment. She and Tinker went home in silence, Tinker said. Around midnight she started to cry, utterly distraught. "I can't do it," she said. "This is the most embarrassing thing; it's going to fall on its face." She was as upset as her husband had ever seen her. "I'd never done what I then did," he said. "I picked up the phone and called, knowing the guys were still there struggling with the rewrite. I called down there and talked to Jim and Allan. I said, 'Mary's hysterical. You guys are not doing it right. Fix it.' "

I didn't have any good advice to give them. I just said, 'fix it.' " He later said that their comments were not reassuring, but when they finally did the shooting on Friday it went remarkably well. They had fixed it. And Moore, by that time, had pulled herself together. "They're [Brooks and Burns] the only ones who know about that phone call," Tinker said, "and I'm the only one who saw this wonderful, dedicated actress going to pieces before my very eyes. The rest of them just saw the professional that she always has been."

Moore had had good reason to be upset. The fortune she and Tinker had invested was riding on the success of the show. They had gone out on a limb for the sitcom—so much so that their nest egg and *The Mary Tyler Moore Show* were, in fact, one entity. Its failure would have destroyed them financially.

That Friday, the obscuring second cameras had been removed, the sound system had been repaired, and a new head of programming at CBS, Fred Silverman, had flown out to see the show (Michael Dann had been fired). Lorenzo Music, the show's story editor, replaced Brooks and Burns for the warm-up with the panache of a stand-up comedian.

At the show's end, Silverman broke the silence on the set by picking up the phone and asking for Robert Wood, the president of CBS. Everyone waited tensely. "Bob," Silverman said. "We have to change the schedules. I've just seen 'The Mary Tyler Moore Show,' and it's a terrific show. We have to move it to Saturday night. . . . I know it's August, and I know it's late, but we've gotta do it because we can't throw this show away." A network schedule had never been changed as late as August, one month before the program was to air. Cast, crew, and technicians could breathe—and shout for joy. The fledgling show had taken flight.

And so on Saturday, September 19, 1970, at 9:30 P.M., *The Mary Tyler Moore Show* aired for the first time and took 37 percent of the market share. But despite its success, it still had a head wind to battle: the critics.

Allan Burns was driving on Melrose Avenue in Los Angeles the day after he had read the show's review in *Time* magazine. He happened to pull up next to Moore in her Jaguar coupe at a stoplight. When he looked over at her he knew she had read the same review. "The look on her face was such devastation," he said. Richard Burgheim had written that the show was "a disaster" for Moore and called Mary Richards "an inadvertent career girl . . . working as a gofer for a drunken clown of a news director . . . an injustice to even the worst of local TV news." Jack Gould had written in the *New York Times,* "Situation comedy fell apart on . . . CBS . . . Mary Tyler Moore is caught in a preposterous item about life as an associate producer in a TV newsroom."

Mary Richards comforts her landlord and friend Phyllis Lindstrom (Cloris Leachman). By the end of its first season, The Mary Tyler Moore Show *had won five Emmy Awards: two for acting (Ed Asner and Valerie Harper), one for directing (Jay Sandrich), and two for writing (Jim Brooks and Allan Burns).*

5

"This Time You're All Alone"

FAITHFULLY AND RELIGIOUSLY, Mary Tyler Moore appeared on Saturday nights, week after week, on television screens across America. Each show began with a montage of shots depicting Mary Richards's life, including a close-up of Mary flashing her broad smile from behind the wheel of her economy-sized car, driving on a crowded highway, as the voice of Sonny Curtis wistfully sings to upbeat music, "How will you make it on your own? This world is awfully big. Girl this time you're all alone." Then follow shots of Mary pulling up to her white Victorian apartment house surrounded by a snow-covered lawn and leafless trees and Mary getting out of her car, gazing at a bridge spanning a lake, symbolic of her crossing from one phase of her life to the next. Mary waves to children sledding nearby; greets a golden retriever and her landlord, Phyllis; sits with her friend Rhoda, chatting happily; and, wearing a fur-trimmed minicoat and high boots, walks through the crowded streets of

Minneapolis looking inquisitive as she carries her groceries. She is her own breadwinner now. Mary hugs Lou Grant, Murray, and Ted at the WJM studio. The song continues in the background, urging Mary Richards to "start living" and avail herself of the love that surrounds her. With that she "might just" succeed.

Mary spins around in the final shot, amid crowds of people in the city, smiling triumphantly as she plucks her blue plaid tam-o'-shanter hat from her head and tosses it in the air, much as Annapolis Naval Academy graduates fling their caps at commencement. In a short sequence of images, the show's producers present Mary as a woman who has graduated from the Laura Petrie kind of housewife dependency and is thrilled to be taking on the world and making it on her own.

Much to the delight of Moore, Tinker, and all of the MTM staff, *The Mary Tyler Moore Show* scored within the top 10 of the Nielsen ratings (the share of an audience for a specific time period, measured by boxes attached to televisions in selected homes to document which channels are watched) throughout the fall of 1970. By the end of its first year it netted five Emmy Awards: two for acting in a supporting role (Ed Asner and Valerie Harper), one for directing (Jay Sandrich), and two for writing (Brooks and Burns).

Through the character of Mary Richards, Moore presented to the world a woman so loving and so giving that in almost every show she would take on the problems of her office mates or friends and, by the show's end, bring them to a happy resolution. Susan Silver, who wrote five scripts reflecting the feminine point of view for the show, referred to Mary Richards as the "hub of a wheel" and to the other characters as its "spokes" rotating around her. In the sixth episode, which aired on October 24, 1970, Mary brings Rhoda and her mother back together after a disagreement. When, in episode 21, "The Boss Isn't Coming to Dinner," Mary learns that Lou and his wife, Edie, are having marital problems because Edie is returning to college, Mary takes Lou's laundry home with her to do. She also accompanies Lou and the men from the

Rhoda listens to her mother (Nancy Walker) during a visit. Moore's character, Mary, often brought Rhoda and Mrs. Morgenstern back together after their numerous arguments.

station to a bar and counters their complaints about women's liberation with wide-eyed, simple logic. "There are no sides," she offers, just lonely men and women. In the end Lou calls Edie and goes home to her.

In the following years, a *Time* magazine reporter wrote, "Someone should write an ode to Mary Tyler Moore, whose show seems to get better with every passing week." Someone actually had written an ode of sorts to Mary during the mak-

Actress Betty White, a close friend of Moore's and Tinker's, plays Sue Ann, the "Happy Homemaker," the host of a cooking show on WJM-TV who shamelessly chases men.

ing of the show's eighth episode, "Divorce Isn't Everything," which aired on October 10, 1970, and featured actor Shelley Berman as a dentist who falls in love with Mary's teeth. Moore began her work that week on Monday morning, bounding with her usual vigor and grace onto the huge Stage 9 at General Service Studios, clad in brown velvet jeans, a suede fringed vest, and an Indian band around her forehead. She grabbed a ringing phone before a sound man could pick it up and chortled, "Good morning, Wanda Wampum here!" Mary, in complete discord with her more groggy fellow stars, baffled the cantankerous Berman. "My God," he complained. "Is she like this every morning?" Moore snatched a seat next to him and kissed him on the cheek. "God you're thin," he said. "You're so thin if I gave you a glass of seltzer water I could see right through you," triggering riotous laughter from Moore. Others around the conference table joined in, and Berman uncharacteristically allowed himself to be caught up in the merriment for the rest of the time he spent with Moore. By the end of that week, Berman, unusually shy, handed Moore a poem he had taken time to write during breaks—a play on her initials:

> Mary to Most
> Of Us
> Is:
> More
> Than
> Most of Us.
> Mary Tyler Moore?
> Mary Tyler MORE.

"More" seemed to have become Moore's motto—she was constantly striving.

Asner wrote of Moore in his 1994 article "Mary & Me" in *New Choices* magazine, "She constantly amazed me with her delight at letting other actors shine as brightly as they could—never limiting anybody in terms of taking their 'star turn.'"

One day on the set during lunch break, while Asner, Gavin MacLeod, Ted Knight, and Jim Brooks played touch football on an adjacent empty lot, Moore and Valerie Harper donned leotards and sweated their way through their three-day-per-week ballet lesson, Harper groaning and Moore gritting her teeth to attain that extra inch of height on her *grand battements,* or high kicks. The workout would be her only moment of "relaxation" during a grueling day of rehearsal for the show. Because Moore was written into almost every scene of each show, she would have to be present and working throughout the day. The lesson over, Moore collapsed into a chair, beads of perspiration draining down her reddened face, lighting cigarette after cigarette of the two packs per day that she smoked. The telephone rang, and Alan Rafkin, who was directing that week's segment, called out jokingly, "Get that, will you, Mary?" As she leaped up to answer the phone he cried, "My God, she thinks I meant it."

Turning to *Good Housekeeping* reporter Muriel Davidson, Rafkin noted that Moore set the pace for everyone in the crew. "There was never any yelling on the set," Rafkin told Davidson. In the show's beginning, "sets didn't roll, props didn't work and dozens of cues were missed by cameramen," he said. "It looked more like a version of 'The Desperate Hours' than 'The Mary Tyler Moore Show,'" Davidson wrote. "But through all the bumbling and the birth pangs . . . Mary seemed calm and contained."

Although little could upset Moore—aside from the disposable lunch trays at the CBS Studios cafeteria that Moore decried for causing more pollution—she did tell Davidson that she was hurt and angry at Hollywood gossip columnist Rona Barrett for referring to her as "the ailing Mary Tyler Moore" because of her diabetes. "That's a terrible thing to do to me," Moore said. "I wouldn't mind so much if she called me 'that rotten actress' . . . or 'the ugly Mary Tyler Moore,' but *ailing!* That's horrible. I've never felt better in my life."

Moore had good reason to feel wonderful by the end of the third season. She was awarded her fourth Emmy, for Best Star in a Leading Comedy Role. In its first two seasons the show had garnered seven Emmy Awards, but none had been bestowed upon Moore until the third season. Malcolm MacPherson of *Newsweek* wrote that Moore knew her business and "looks good while she's doing it." Moore, self-deprecatingly, replied that her strength lay not in "being funny," but "in reacting in a funny way to those around her." MacPherson did, however, call Mary Richards a "goody two-shoes," a "square," and "slightly uptight." In response, writers for the show would later enliven Mary's dating life. In one episode, Mary's visiting mother would tell Mary's father to remember to take his pill, and Mary would answer absently,

"OK," letting the audience know that she is taking an oral contraceptive.

By the beginning of the show's fourth season, in September 1973, Mary began to show even more signs of change. She no longer wore her dark brown hair in a long and bouncy flip; instead she wore it shorter and curled under, and she colored it a reddish brown, as women often do to cover signs of graying. She replaced her chipper naïveté with a more sedate, mature demeanor. Most of all, she had a new and striking air of assertiveness that would bring her closer to the role-model ideal of the liberated woman making it in a man's world, for which so many women admired her. In episode number 73, "The Lars

Moore and Tinker attend the Emmy Awards ceremony on May 20, 1973, during which she won the award for Best Actress in a Television Series for The Mary Tyler Moore Show. *Moore and Tinker seldom entertained and neither had close friends of their own. They began to take each other for granted, and in November 1973 they decided to separate.*

News director Lou Grant and anchorman Ted Baxter try to comfort Mary during an episode in which the usually cheerful Mary is depressed. On the same evening that Moore separated from Tinker, she had to film the episode in which Lou Grant separates from his wife, Edie, and has to decide whether to sell his house. Moore later commented, "I'm kind of strange, the harder it is for me the stronger I am."

Affair," Phyllis discovers that her husband, Lars (an unseen character), is having an affair with a new character on the show, Sue Ann, played by veteran actress Betty White, a personal friend of Moore and Tinker. Sue Ann embodies bitchiness with a smile and flagrantly chases men. She is the hostess of WJM's *Happy Homemaker* show, and she is not at all shy about her new conquest. Phyllis, representing the as-yet-unliberated housewife, unfamiliar with assertiveness, comes to Mary's office one day to employ her support while she confronts Sue Ann about her impropriety. Torn between work and friendship, Mary consents to give her a few minutes and then hangs around in the background of the *Happy Homemaker* set while from behind her TV kitchen counter frilly-aproned Sue Ann ignores Phyllis's pathetic plea to stop seeing her husband. Finally Phyllis, near tears, turns to Mary for help. In a breakthrough moment, Mary integrates her anger, assertiveness, and loyalty to her friend as she explodes in a burst of moral outrage. She steps between Phyllis and Sue Ann, close to Sue Ann's face, narrows her usually fawnlike eyes, leans her head forward, and in a no-nonsense, bottom-line, businesslike way delivers a high-speed verbal thrashing, hardly taking a breath:

> Sue Ann, listen to me because I've got to be in the screening room in 45 seconds. Ted already knows about this thing with you and Lars. You know what a big mouth he has. And what Ted doesn't tell, I will tell, and pretty soon it's going to be all over the station. And they're not going to think that that's a terrific image for the "Happy Homemaker," so you see it comes down to a choice: either Lars or your show. I've gotta go now. [To Phyllis] I will see you later.

With that, Mary marches out of the set, leaving Sue Ann flabbergasted and defeated and giving Phyllis just enough nerve to smear Sue Ann's chocolate mousse all over her white apron, eliciting a burst of audience applause and cheers. Phyllis and Lars stay together.

Moore's own life with Grant Tinker gave her even more satisfaction in the first year of her show than did her work. Looking back on that time, Tinker told reporter Vernon Scott, "Everything in our marriage went smoothly then." Tinker was working on the new MTM production *The Bob Newhart Show*, about a psychiatrist, his wife, and his patients, and he was making plans for Valerie Harper to have her own sitcom called *Rhoda*. Tinker and Moore had two homes: an apartment in Malibu, an exclusive oceanfront community near Hollywood, California, and a rambling colonial-style home in Beverly Hills. Moore rode to work in her Rolls Royce each day and came home at 6:00 P.M. to her three dogs—Max, a German shepherd, and Maude and Diswilliam, two gray miniature poodles. She would have a cocktail to relax, read her scripts, or busy herself with odd jobs such as putting new ribbons in her ballet shoes. In the evenings, after Tinker arrived home from his long day at work, the two would dine by candlelight and promptly fall asleep from exhaustion afterward.

But Moore and Tinker had little in their lives outside their spheres of work—little they could bring to the marriage. They entertained rarely, and neither had many close friends of their own. Because they were both private people they did not admit their inner thoughts and feelings to one another, and in time, they came to take each other for granted. "We realized that something was missing in our relationship," Moore told Vernon Scott. "Tempers frayed. There were outbursts for no apparent reason." One night when Tinker, suffering from a migraine headache, could not sleep, he mentioned to Moore that he wished he had a hobby to keep his mind occupied. She suggested mending crippled birds.

Their lack of communication showed itself most clearly in the building of a magnificent house in Malibu. Each had thought the other wanted it, but in fact, neither did.

Moore was delighted to have won another Emmy, for Outstanding Continued Performance by an Actress in a Leading Role in a Comedy Series for the 1972–73 season, but by the following season, by Thanksgiving 1973, she and Tinker were discussing separation. "It was damned painful," Moore told Scott. "I loved Grant so much." Finally Moore said it was time, and Tinker moved into a small house high in the Hollywood hills. Ironically, the day he left, Friday, November 30, Moore had to entertain British journalists. One said to her, "Tell me, Mary, how is it that you have such a marvelous marriage?" Dan Jenkins, Moore's public relations person at the time, said Moore gave all the "right" answers, but when it came time for them to leave, she rose and "put her hand to her mouth, kind of choking back a sob."

To make matters worse, that night Moore was filming the episode in which Lou Grant faces separation from Edie. He had to decide whether to sell the house. "I was bothered by the story content," Moore told Scott. "But I'm kind of strange, the harder it is for me the stronger I am." After her performance that night, Jim Brooks embraced Moore to console her as tears streamed down her face. Some observers mistook his gesture for more than friendly support, and false rumors of an affair spread.

Moore did not tell the cast about her separation from Tinker until a week later. When she finally did, some said it felt like being told as a child that one's parents have separated.

Divorce, that taboo subject that almost sank *The Mary Tyler Moore Show* at its inception, now came of age within the show and loomed all too menacingly in the life of its brilliant star, Mary Tyler Moore. At 37, Moore herself seemed to be facing the prospect of making it all on her own.

In March 1974, Moore and Tinker are caught in a moment of private conversation during the International Broadcasting Awards party. After six weeks apart the couple reconciled. Moore observed, "Much as we want to please the person we love, we must never please to the point of totally erasing ourselves. There's got to be an otherness in marriage."

6

"A Long Way to Tipperary"

MOORE'S KITCHEN COUNTER faced the Pacific Ocean in her new Malibu home, giving her a panoramic view of the sunsets and all the beach activity. But because she was alone, she "began not to see it anymore," to take it for granted, she told Vernon Scott. Moore concluded that was what had happened to her marriage with Tinker—they had taken each other for granted.

She continued with her life apart from him—unhappily, but trying not to show it. Reporter Joyce Maynard, writing for *McCall's* magazine, described Moore at this time: "In spite of her separation her life seems to be in order . . . she appears to be in control of things . . . whether she is or not, the appearance of order will, at all costs, be maintained." Moore's secretary, Prasuti, noted that Moore would never want to inflict her problems on anyone. But despite her fierce determination to keep up appearances, Moore showed some signs of stress. She dieted more than usual—obsessively, noting at one point, "I really should lose two more pounds" and claiming that her size-three pants were "too tight." One friend observed that Moore would keep putting more gum into her mouth until her cheeks "puffed up like a chipmunk's." Sadly, in an oddly prescient comment, Prasuti noted that she could not picture Moore sitting on the floor in an encounter group telling everybody in the circle what she really thought of them; instead, she pictured Moore sitting in an armchair in a corner, watching and doing her needlepoint.

Rather than discuss her separation from Tinker, Moore simply dismissed it as "a private matter between two people" and focused, instead, on Mary Richards and social issues. "I was on a panel once, discussing 'women and television' with Gloria Steinem [editor of the feminist magazine *Ms.* and a leading spokesperson for the women's liberation movement] and several women's liberationists," Moore told Maynard. Women in the audience asked Moore why she did not use her position in the show to insist on more scripts dealing with women's rights. "Well I believe in them," Moore answered, "and we'll always sneak things in where we can, but the show isn't about furthering causes, and if it were, it wouldn't be funny." Moore concluded by saying that the show was really about six characters and their relationships.

Moore also threw herself into her charity work, helping such organizations as the Cleveland Amory Fund for Animals and Los Ranchos Amigos, a hospital for bedridden children.

And then there was her son, Richie. In 1969, Moore had sent him to a private school in Arizona to keep him away from the drug-infested schools in Los Angeles. Now 17 years old, he lived with his father and stepmother in Fresno, California, at his request. Despite this fact, Moore told reporter Tracey Johnston of the *New York Times* that they had a "very close relationship."

Moore kept a portrait of Richie on the wall of her immovable dressing room trailer that was kept impeccably neat. On a nearby bookshelf, a book entitled *What to Do About Our Teenagers* prompted a question from a reporter about how

In Washington, D.C., in 1975, critic Cleveland Amory (left) and Moore, who holds a fox trap, testify before a House subcommittee considering a bill that would outlaw types of animal traps thought to be inhumane. Moore is involved in women's-rights causes and in numerous charities, including the Cleveland Amory Fund for Animals and Los Ranchos Amigos (a hospital for children).

Ted gives his opinion when Mary is confronted with going to jail for refusing to reveal a news source in a 1974 episode. Throughout the course of the series, the character Mary Richards became more independent as a woman and more powerful in the workplace.

she raised Richie. Was she strict? Yes, she acknowledged, she was a strict mother. "We tend to repeat what our own parents have done, I think," she said. "I had a fairly strict Catholic upbringing, and Richie's upbringing has reflected that." Moore went on to say that Richie was the only kid on his block without a skateboard. "I've loosened up some now," Moore said of her relationship with Richie. "If somebody had said to me five years ago that my son would choose to go with his father, I would have felt like a failure," she said. "Now I've come to realize that the time comes when you've just got to let go."

As the weeks passed during her separation from Tinker, Moore found it difficult to distract herself from the separation by working or dancing, but when she did she still derived satisfaction from both. She told a reporter that managing to memorize a page-long speech for the show in only one night, and then being able to deliver it really fast—"you know, the kind where you don't even stop to breathe?"—gave her the feeling of "well, sort of like watching the Rockettes. And I'm happy when I'm dancing," she added. As she worked through the highly disciplined movements of ballet to calming piano music she found a sort of "cheap form of therapy," she said. "When you're hurting—physically hurting—you can't think about your problems," she added.

Moore could avoid her feelings about Tinker for only so long, however. During their separation, she and Tinker called each other about business matters more than they really needed to, and Tinker offered advice on how to squelch the rumors about her and Jim Brooks. At one point, Moore called Tinker to say that she was "hurting so much and going through such a terrible time" that she wanted to talk to him about it because he was her "best friend." Tinker *was* her best friend—her only real friend—she told Scott. Moore added that Tinker was the only person she ever confided in and that the separation was the most painful thing she had ever gone through.

Tinker was luckier in a sense. He could bury himself in long hours of work, but he admitted that at the time he did become a loner. Both he and Moore insisted that there were no other lovers in their lives. The problem lay solely between the two of them.

At Christmas 1973 they were still apart. Moore traveled to Puerto Rico with friends, "determined" to have fun, but the soothing white beaches and the clear water of the Caribbean Sea could not take her mind off Tinker. He remained alone at his mountain retreat, surrounded by Christmas presents— including Moore's, a handmade needlepoint-covered appointment book—none of which he could bring himself to open.

Finally in mid-January, after six weeks of separation, Moore received an impersonal note from Tinker concerning the show. It was addressed "Mary" and signed "Grant." "I hated that because it wasn't us," Moore told Scott. "It was one of the ways I knew whether we would get a divorce or not— changing the *us* feeling we'd shared for twelve years." Because of the note, Moore called him to say she did not think they were communicating very well. Tinker broke the ice with an invitation to dinner, and Moore accepted, although she was afraid they had not had enough time apart. She met him in the studio parking lot and he offered to show her his "little house" and then take her to dinner. While they were having a drink at Tinker's house, their friend Allen Ludden, Betty White's husband, called to invite Tinker to a birthday party for Ludden the following night, so Tinker asked Moore to accompany him; she accepted, and he said he would go to her show that night, too.

"My attitude at the time I asked her for that first date was the response to a deep-felt need," Tinker told Scott. "It seemed like the right time to reestablish our marriage." He added, "I didn't want to lose Mary."

After several dates, Moore frequented Tinker's rented house. Eventually they decided to put the beach house up for sale. Their mutual interest in MTM, along with their love for each other, had brought them back together. Moore, reflecting on the split and the reconciliation, told Scott that she did most of the growing during their separation. She had to come to grips with her identity and her needs as a star. Accustomed to deference and attention, she realized that she had to change her attitude. She recalled a night after their reconciliation when she directed her first episode of *The Mary Tyler Moore Show*; Tinker said, "Hey, that was terrific," kissed her, but then returned to discussion with the producers. Moore wanted to get his feedback on details of the show, but Tinker remained in conference. Frustrated, Moore finally told herself not to be a "Sarah Star. I had to be mature enough to realize his problems are just as important as the big days in my own life. I wasn't hurt," she said, "but I would have been before the separation."

Sitting in Tinker's office at CBS Studio Center, Moore, wearing a light-blue sweater and white pants, lit a cigarette and grinned uneasily at Tinker as she offered her own newly developed views on marriage: "I think holding something back, keeping a few things private just for yourself, is a very important part of being who you are," she said. "Much as we want to please the person we love, we must never please to the point of totally erasing ourselves. There's got to be an *otherness* in marriage."

Moore stressed the importance of the woman being strong "now and then. . . . If you've confessed all your foibles and fears, and you've sobbed it all out, then how are you ever going to be strong for him when he needs strength?" she asked.

Moore and Tinker were a couple again. Their 13-year marriage, minus six weeks, had survived. The actors and staff of *The Mary Tyler Moore Show,* who had considered them mother and father figures of the project, heaved a collective sigh of relief.

Moore and Tinker had more than one reason to celebrate after their reunion. By 1974, critics had come to extol not only *The Mary Tyler Moore Show* but Moore herself. Cyclops, a pen name for one of the toughest critics, wrote, "If

only both of us weren't married to someone else." Frederick
A. Birmingham of the *Saturday Evening Post* revealed that he
was equally smitten, describing himself as a bumbling, fum-
bling lovesick boy over Moore, and another tough critic,
Cleveland Amory of *TV Guide*, awarded Moore his personal
Emmy. *Time* magazine, which had panned the first episode,
now wrote that the show had turned the usual "brass" of sit-
coms into "something resembling gold." James Stewart-
Gordon summed up the public's sentiments in *Reader's
Digest:* "Everybody loves . . . Mary."

Perry Lafferty, vice president of programming for CBS in
Hollywood, sought to explain Moore's appeal in an interview
with *New York Times Magazine* writer Tracey Johnston.
"Well, she's the well scrubbed, all American girl that everyone likes," he said, commenting that her "vulnerability" made
her so appealing. She is like a "little girl lost," he said. "Also,
she's beautiful without being threatening." By that he meant
not too sexy. In 1974, Americans were uncomfortable with a
woman who was too sexy appearing on weekly television,
according to Lafferty. He explained that it would raise "all the
id-like elements [basic human appetites] inside people" and
they would not know how to deal with them. "Don't forget,"
he continued, "the TV audience is different from the film
audience. It won't take change in the characters." Johnston,
however, concluded that men "whose taste in women run
from [country music singer] Tammy Wynette to Gloria
Steinem" believed Moore would make "the perfect girlfriend," while women liked the fact that she was a star without being a sex queen. Mothers liked her even though
Moore's character spent a night with a man and was taking
the pill. In short, Johnston joined the chorus of Moore's
admirers, writing, "She may, in fact, be the most well liked
woman in America."

Mary Tyler Moore's appeal was not limited to the average American. Sophisticates now numbered among the
show's 31 million viewers. Daniel Menaker wrote in the *New
York Times* that Moore was so "in" that it had become fash-

When Mr. Grant and Mary go on a date in an episode aired in 1977, Mr. Grant has a dream about Mary and visualizes that this is how she would look on their golden wedding anniversary. The two colleagues and friends realize that a relationship would never work, and finally Mary is able to call her boss by his first name, Lou.

ionable to "drift into the den at a party—or go home—at 9 on Saturday night because you 'simply must not miss' her program." The *New Yorker* published a cartoon of a man drooling over her, and a female sociology professor at the University of California said that she watched the show Saturday nights when she was alone "and therefore morose" because it was the only show that was not offensive to women, and she also appreciated the friendship of Mary and Rhoda.

But critics and intellectuals alone do not determine ratings. Fans do. Among them, Moore found some her most ardent supporters. One woman wrote:

> Thank you for Mary Richards. I am 35, unmarried and not looking very hard. Since your program came on the air, people have begun to understand that there is a life for women like me. Married friends have stopped being patronizing; some are even a bit envious!

Asked about all the hoopla surrounding her show, Moore told Johnston that if she thought about it "it would drive me bananas." She added that she did the show primarily for her friends and colleagues.

By October 1974, *The Mary Tyler Moore Show* had won 16 Emmy Awards and ranked among the nation's top seven entertainments. Moore walked away from the Emmy Awards presentation with two statues, one for Best Lead Actress in a Comedy Series and one for Actress of the Year—Series. By then, an older, wiser Moore appeared in the show's fifth-season opening montage to different lyrics sung by Sonny Curtis. Mary walks briskly along a lake as Curtis sings: "Who can turn the world on with her smile?" instead of "How will you make it on your own?" He continues, "Who can take a nothing day and suddenly make it all seem worth while?" Curtis answers, "Well it's you girl and you should know it, with each glance and every little movement you show it. Love is all around." Most important, Mary is shown on the job, holding a microphone to a policeman as her crew films an on-the-spot take while people crowd around to watch. Mary is no longer Lou Grant's glorified secretary.

Amid the riotous comedy that was standard fare each week, Mary grew as a woman and as a professional. In episode 97, "Will Mary Go to Jail?" Mary refuses to reveal her news source and faces jail. She cries out to Lou, "I know it's the right thing to do. There's just one problem, Mr.

Grant—I don't want to go to jail!" But off she goes, sharing her cell with several prostitutes who provide exceptionally funny contrast to the conservative Mary. Later, in episode 117, "When You Try to Be a Nice Guy," one of the prostitutes, played by Barbara Colby, reappears, asking Mary to sponsor her while she applies for a job so that she does not have to go back to jail. Mary, of course, does so, and the prostitute lands several jobs, including one as a fashion designer. Mary demonstrates in this show that her generosity extends beyond the spheres of her friends and colleagues to those of the most socially outcast. Writer Michael Leeson did not miss an opportunity for humor, though, giving Mary the job of modeling an exceedingly tacky and sexy outfit for, of all people, crusty Lou.

In episode 112, Mary pursues the job of producing the news, with hilarious results. Nevertheless, Mary Richards has continued to seek autonomy and power in the workplace. Her greatest move forward— from Lou Grant's daughter figure to his equal—comes when, in episode 167, she asks Lou on a date. Richards demonstrates her own moral code through her disgust when, earlier in the show, her previous date starts to take off his clothes while she makes coffee. In one of her few angry tirades, Mary chides the man and decries all her years of dating, which have come to nothing. With Ted Baxter's wife, Georgette, giving her a push, she "grentions" and "fumphers" her way through the dinner invitation to Lou. Their actual date, during which they have dinner at Mary's apartment, proves even more nerve-racking for both of them, until they finally burst out laughing when they try to kiss. Relieved, the two good friends acknowledge that the relationship would never work. Mary, however, has reached a milestone in finally being able to call her gruff but lovable father figure and boss by his first name, signaling her growth and her final achievement of equality in the workplace.

The 1976–77 television season was to be the last for *The Mary Tyler Moore Show*. All the players had decided that it was best to conclude the series while they were still ahead.

In the last episode of The Mary Tyler Moore Show, *which aired on March 19, 1977, Ted tries to console Lou and Mary after they are told that everyone, except Ted, has been fired from the news station. To keep the cast and crew from actually crying during the filming of "The Last Show," a producer placed actors dressed as American Indians with deadpan faces behind the cast during rehearsal.*

Betty White told writers Robert Alley and Irby Brown that Moore came to work on the first day of the season saying, "This is the first day of the week of the last year," and that the feeling went on every day all year long. "Everybody knew something magic was drawing to a close," White said.

The story line for the last show called for the entire WJM crew—except for Ted Baxter, ironically—to be fired by the new station manager. Rhoda had left for her own spin-off show in 1974, and Phyllis had left the following year for hers. After Richards and the others learn of the bad news, Lou secretly arranges for Rhoda and Phyllis to come back to Minneapolis, where he takes them to visit Mary at her apartment. Comically, Phyllis vies with Rhoda to see who can console Mary first, as Mary falls crying into their arms. In keeping with the show's strong theme of affection among the characters, Phyllis asks Mary to go with her to San Francisco, where she now lives, and Rhoda suggests New York, her new home.

Director Jay Sandrich would lead the cast to an Emmy Award–winning performance in the show that aired March 19, 1977. *The Mary Tyler Moore Show* itself won an Emmy for Outstanding Comedy Series that year, and Allan Burns, Jim Brooks, Ed Weinberger, Stan Daniels, David Lloyd, and Bob Ellison, the show's producers over its seven-year run, won an Emmy for their cowritten script of "The Last Show."

Lloyd told of their immediate problem during rehearsals and filming of "The Last Show": how to keep the cast and crew from becoming weepy. Weinberger solved the problem. At that time a Western was being filmed on the MTM lot, so he got actors dressed in full American Indian regalia and seated them, unknown to Moore, at desks in the back of the newsroom where extras usually sat. When Moore came out to do a scene, she found she was getting laughs from the audience of 40 or so people who worked on the show—in the wrong places. She realized they were enjoying something that she was missing, so she turned around and saw all the Indians with their unsmiling faces. "And it blew her away," Lloyd said. She was all right for the remainder of the rehearsal; there was "no danger of her suddenly becoming too emotional."

In the show's final scene, Mary Richards says to her fellow WJM crew members gathered in the newsroom:

> Well, I wanted you to know that sometimes I get concerned about being a career woman. I get to thinking my job is too important to me, and I tell myself that the people I work with are just the people I work with. And not my family. And last night, I thought what is a family anyway? They're just people who make you feel less alone and really loved. And that's what you've done for me. Thank you for being my family.

With that, they all embrace and slowly maneuver out of the newsroom as one large clump of hugging "family." Brooks said, "That's good, but we need to get a laugh."

According to Ed Asner, "Someone in our huddle—I don't even recall who—said, 'Well, we're crying. We could get a tissue or something.' Jim Brooks said, 'Well, could the tissue box be on the desk? Can you, without letting go of each other, move en masse to get it?' The group did, looking like an enormous centipede, and it worked. The tears were there, but we also got the wonderful, rich laugh we needed."

There was a danger that the actors might break out of their roles and reveal their real pain in that scene, Lloyd said. Bob Ellison remembered that Moore had once said that there was something impressive and even appealing about men in military uniforms, so as the producers tried to think of ways to avoid overemotionalism, Weinberger brought that up. Ellison went to a wardrobe man for a uniform, and he borrowed a monocle from an actor friend. "I looked like something in 'Hogan's Heroes' [a sitcom about Allied servicemen in a World War II German prisoner-of-war camp]," he said. He could not get himself to put on the uniform pants, thinking a Nazi might have worn them, so instead he got a pair of boxer shorts to complete the outfit.

Moore had just been introduced to the audience, as she was before the filming of each show. "It was so difficult for her," Lloyd said. She took her bow and went back offstage, tears streaming down her face. Just then she saw Ellison and, in relief, jumped into his arms. "That relieved the problem for a few minutes," Lloyd said.

By the show's end, when Mary Richards had delivered her speech and she, Lou, Murray, Sue Ann, Ted, and Georgette began their slow move to the door, quietly they began to sing the World War I song "It's a Long Way to Tipperary," an idea of Jim Brooks's during rehearsal. Softly they sang:

> It's a long way to Tipperary.
> It's a long way to go.
> It's a long way to Tipperary,
> to the sweetest girl I know.
> Farewell Tipperary.
> Farewell Leicester Square.
> It's a long, long way to Tipperary,
> But my heart's still there.

As incongruous as the song may have seemed, it spoke to the sadness of being parted from that which was dearest, a sadness that the actors and crew seemed to feel as keenly as soldiers in a faraway land might feel. Moore and the others would have to go on with their own lives, to unknown artistic ventures, with no guarantee of success, and with no assurance of the harmonious working atmosphere that had reigned on the set of *The Mary Tyler Moore Show* for seven happy years.

All that remained after the last show was a commemorative plaque at the entrance to Sound Stage 2 that read:

> On this stage
> a company of loving
> and talented friends
> produced
> a television classic,
>
> Mary Tyler Moore
> Show
> 1970–1977

A pensive-looking Mary Tyler Moore. After her long-running series, audiences tended to identify the actress with her sweet, effervescent character Mary Richards. But in reality, Moore's life was filled with pain.

7

TRAGEDY AND TRIUMPH

SUCCESS ELUDED MOORE in her next venture, a series of television variety shows, but failure hardly prepared her for a far-greater loss to come. In February 1978, one year after the end of *The Mary Tyler Moore Show,* Moore's sister Elizabeth took her own life. Despondent over a failed love affair, at the age of 21 she took an overdose of the pain-killing medication Darvon. Moore learned of Elizabeth's death from Tinker, who supported her as she tried to comfort her mother.

Moore drew on her own tragedy to portray a survivor of breast cancer in the television special *First, You Cry,* based on journalist and author Betty Rollin's own experience. Grant Tinker had given Moore the book, and after reading the first three chapters, she had decided she wanted to play the part. "It was the first dramatic role I'd played in years and years, and I wasn't sure I could bring enough colors—feelings—to it," she told a reporter. Moore performed so well that the reviewers were ecstatic, the

At the funeral of Moore's sister Elizabeth, who committed suicide at age 21. From left: actress Cloris Leachman, Grant Tinker, an unidentified friend, and Mary Tyler Moore.

ratings were high, and she received an Emmy Award nomination.

In April 1979, *The Mary Tyler Moore Hour* aired on CBS, and Moore attempted to bounce back from the low ratings of her first variety show with a series of comedy hours in which she played the character Mary McKinnon. The critics panned the program and it was canceled.

But Moore soon faced another setback.

Despite their efforts to grow and strengthen their marriage, by December 1979—after 16 years—Moore and Tinker parted for good. It was Moore's decision. She told reporter Jeff Rovin, "Our relationship was that of a father to a child." Four years earlier Moore had declared it was "chauvinistic for men to think they are the more important member of a family" but had conceded, "That's the kind of marriage we have . . . an old-world relationship." By 1979, however, Moore had outgrown that kind of relationship, just as Mary Richards had outgrown the father/daughter relationship she had had with Lou Grant.

Until that point, Moore and Tinker had been living in a house in Bel Air, an affluent residential section of Los Angeles. She sold the house to Tinker and moved east to live in the Waldorf Towers in New York City. With no job to go to each day, "the going was very rough for her," Tinker later told reporter L. A. Lague. "Her cool head was not enough." Moore turned to alcohol to help her ease the pain of the divorce. Even before then, Moore had relied on drinking. Still, "she's cautious," a friend said. "I've never seen her sloshed, just a little high."

Moore's difficulty adjusting to her new single life was compounded by her inexperience in getting close to anyone other than Tinker. In Los Angeles she had not pursued close relationships. "I wasn't the first to open up," she told one reporter, "thus I had more colleagues than friends. I never really allowed anybody to know me." Moore felt she would "burden people" if she shared her "darkest and saddest moments," she said. "I had to learn to do what people did at 22," she said. So she began to broaden her horizons, making new friends, eventually moving to an apartment on Manhattan's Upper West Side.

Professionally, Moore took on new roles that called for her to plunge into the depths of what she called her "dark side"—that private, insecure part of herself that she had kept hidden from the world throughout her entire life. Her recent sadness weighed more heavily on that aspect of herself, making it almost impossible for her to play forever-chipper types of roles. It was Moore's time to grow as an actress and to develop characters of greater depth and scope than Mary Richards or Laura Petrie.

Ironically, her first great role was that of housewife Beth Jarrett in the 1980 Academy Award–winning movie *Ordinary People*. Moore's portrayal of a woman emotionally jarred by the drowning death of her son raised her above the level of television sitcom award winner to a nomination for Best Actress by the American Academy of Motion Picture Arts and Sciences. Moore, in the character of Beth Jarrett, showed the world what could—and most probably did—go on in the life of a woman so like herself: impeccably neat, cheery to all in her country club milieu, yet cold and emotionally constricted toward her teenage son Connie (played by Timothy Hutton), who remains guilt-stricken and mentally scarred by surviving the sailing accident that claimed his brother's life. Most strikingly, Beth is a woman who can love the son who died because he was so unlike her (he was rugged and athletic), while she cannot give love to Connie, who resembles her in his sensitivity and his tendency to withhold his feelings from others. Through intense psychotherapy Connie learns to get in touch with his feelings of guilt, sorrow, and anger toward his alienated parents. He is able to bring his father, Cal (played by Donald Sutherland), to understand his plight, but in doing so he also makes Cal see Beth's inability to move outside of herself to meet both Connie's and his own needs. In a scene that is shocking for its departure from the Mary Richards persona, Moore, as Beth, explodes with rage at Cal on a golf course when he suggests that they include Connie in their future vacations. Beth accuses Cal of blaming her for their older son Buck's death and for Connie's subsequent suicide attempt. Cal asks her whether she can see things in any way other than how they affect her.

> *Beth:* No, I can't [yelling]. Neither can you; neither can anybody else. Maybe I'm just a little more honest about it.
>
> *Cal:* Well stop being so goddamned hones and start being a little generous and start thinking about him for a while.
>
> *Beth:* I don't know what he expects from me. I never have known.
>
> *Cal:* Well I'll tell you what he expects.
>
> *Beth:* What? He wants me to throw my arms around him every time he passes an exam? I cannot respond when someone says, "Here, I just did this great thing. Love me."
>
> *Cal:* I'll tell you what he wants. All he wants is to know that you don't hate him. That's it.
>
> *Beth:* God! how could I hate him? Mothers don't hate their sons...God! I dont' know what anyone wants from me anymore.

When Beth's brother interjects, "We just want you to be happy," she shoots back, every sinew of her lean body taut like a coil about to spring, her face contorted bitterly,

"Happy? Ward, you tell me the definition of happy, huh? But first you better be good and sure that your kids are good and safe. That no one's fallen off a horse or been hit by a car or drowned in the swimming pool you're so proud of!"

As Cal looks on, angry and ashamed, Beth closes with, "And then you come to me and tell me how to be happy," emphasizing each word.

Later, on a plane going home from their vacation, the camera closes in on Beth's face, in deep, despondent contemplation. Later still, at home one night, Cal confronts her, telling her she is "so determined," but she is not "strong." He asks her whether she loves him, and then goes on to say she "can't handle mess. You need everything neat and easy. Maybe you can't love anybody." He goes on, "When Buck died you buried all your love with him, and I don't understand that. I just don't know. Maybe it wasn't even Buck. Maybe it was just you."

Beth's expression reveals a glimmer of disbelief. "Finally it was the best of you that you buried," he says. "But whatever it was, I don't know who you are." Cal concludes that he does not love Beth anymore. With that she bites her lip; her eyes water, she turns away, goes upstairs into her room, pulls a suitcase down from the closet shelf, and packs her bag to leave. She slowly begins to shudder, building from a tremor to full quaking. In the end, Beth leaves.

The film ends with Cal and Connie hugging and finally telling each other—for the first time in Connie's life—that they love each other.

Moore said that the film's director, Robert Redford (renowned for his many film performances, including *Butch Cassidy and the Sundance Kid* and *The Sting*), "cast me in *Ordinary People* because he had long suspected there was a dark side to Mary Tyler Moore. . . . We all have our dark sides, maybe especially those of us who are sunny and shiny-faced." Redford told L. A. Lague that it "took courage" for Moore to play Beth Jarrett. "Beth is Mary, the small frightened person inside the big daring person, the person who clutches for control, who won't play the game unless she can make the rules." Redford went on to say, "In playing Beth, Mary faced that side of herself and lived it out—brilliantly. I'm really in awe of her."

As much as Moore was lauded for her portrayal of sunny, independent Mary Richards, she was praised for her role in a film that broke new ground in the motion picture industry. *Ordinary People* entered the living rooms of the very type of American family that felt compelled to hide its dark side—its feelings of anguish and turmoil—from the world. *Ordinary People* made it acceptable for families, not only of the upper middle class but of all classes, to deal with subjects like psychotherapy, alienation, and family trauma more openly than ever before.

Tragedy followed on the heels of Moore's great film success in a horribly ironic way. Like Beth Jarrett, she too lost a beloved son. In October 1980, during the release of *Ordinary People,* Moore received an early-morning phone call from Tinker. It was a call he had waited five hours to make—a call he hated to make—knowing it would shatter what calm Moore held onto in her life. Police had told him that Richie had died of a self-inflicted gunshot wound. It was 2:30 A.M. eastern standard time on October 15 when Tinker received the news. He did not want to wake Moore. "It was the hardest thing I ever had to do," he said later.

Richie had been living in a rented house with two roommates near the University of Southern California campus. He had collected guns and enjoyed target shooting. On Tuesday night, October 14, 1980, while talking on the telephone to his girlfriend in Fresno, California, he had been loading and unloading his shotgun. Then at 11:10 P.M., while talking to one of his roommates, he accidentally hit the trigger and shot himself in the face. He was rushed to the hospital, where he died soon after. "At no time did he seem despondent," his roommate, 23-year-old Janet McLaughlin, a student at the University of Southern California, reported. Richie's death was ruled accidental by a coroner's investigation.

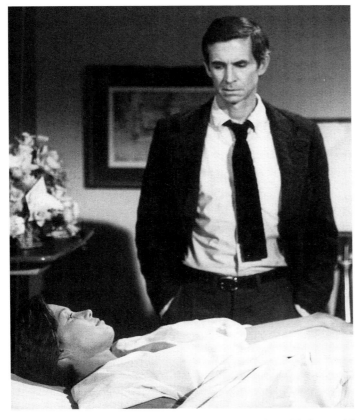

Moore and actor Anthony Perkins in the television movie First, You Cry, *which aired on November 8, 1978. Moore played a woman struggling to cope with breast cancer.*

Moore flew to Los Angeles the next day. Tinker told reporters that she was "absolutely destroyed."

Moore's "sometimes troubled relationship" with Richie had been improving. After drifting for several years, her 24-year-old son had landed a job in a CBS mail room. For Moore, as she later told a reporter, it was as though a benevolent God had lied.

Moore went into seclusion following Richie's death. She saw only close friends and a therapist. In time, however, she found the most important thing for her in dealing with his death was "talking, talking, and talking to people who offered their ears." Later she told Valerie Harper, "I have my times. It's been really horrible, and sometimes I cry for hours, but, my God, people have had a lot worse than I have."

Yet Moore's losses mounted. In 1981 she and Tinker ended their 18-year marriage by divorcing.

Stoically, Moore prevailed after Richie's death and her divorce. She went on to pursue her career on the stage, attempting to reverse her failure there so many years before in *Breakfast at Tiffany's*. This time she took on a role as challenging as that of Beth Jarrett, one that allowed her to tap into her own suffering. She played a quadriplegic (a person paralyzed from the neck down) in Brian Clark's play *Whose Life Is It Anyway?*, produced by Emanual Azenburg in New York. Moore played a part originally written for a man, replacing Tom Conti, who won a Tony Award for his portrayal of Ken Harrison. As Claire Harrison, Moore was a sculptor who wanted to be allowed to die since she was unable to move. *Newsweek* critic Jack Kroll wrote in March 1980 that Moore did "a solid, professional and appealing job of acting" in the role. She was given an honorary Tony Award for her portrayal of Claire Harrison.

As Moore improved onstage, turning the dross of her personal tragedies into gold, the God whom she thought would reward her for living a good life and doing good things

Robert Redford, in his directorial debut, confers with Moore on the set of Ordinary People. *The acclaimed movie featured Moore in a different kind of role—as a cold, emotionally barren wife and mother.*

seemed to be driving her ever closer to the edge of despair. But Moore doggedly fought back. In 1982, Moore's mother had a stroke (a blockage of blood flow to a part of the brain that can result in partial, temporary, or permanent paralysis). At the same time, her father was hospitalized for 43 days with an abdominal aneurysm (a pathological blood-filled dilation of a blood vessel). Moore offered her parents a trip to Europe "as a carrot if they both recover[ed]." Her incentive worked, and Moore and her parents headed off on their tour of London, Paris, Rome, Vienna, Venice, and the south of France. Through her work as an American liaison for Daytop Village, an American organization against drug abuse, which had just turned international, Moore obtained an audience with Pope John Paul II, who said a private mass for Moore, her parents, and nine other people at his summer residence, Castel Gandolfo. Following the mass, the pope met with each person separately in his antechamber. Moore reported later that she could see the brim of her black hat trembling during mass. "It was the transcendent experience of the trip," she said, "and I think of all our lives. It went beyond material experience: it was soul touching."

Soon after Moore and her parents returned from Europe, her mother developed severe bronchitis. Mrs. Moore's doctor was unavailable, so Moore spoke to Dr. S. Robert Levine, who was taking his colleague's calls. Moore noticed that Levine, a handsome 29-year-old cardiologist, seemed especially sensitive to her mother. When she took her mother to the hospital, Levine impressed her even more with his tenderness, caring, and humor while he examined Mrs. Moore. He admitted her mother to the hospital, and Mary, exhausted from the trip and having palpitations, asked Levine to listen to her heart. "You're just nervous," he told her. "Relax!" Three days later Levine discharged Mrs. Moore and gave Mary his telephone number to call in case of an emergency. "Does loneliness count?" she asked. "Yes," he answered with a smile.

A few nights later, on September 30, 1982, Moore, alone in her luxurious Central Park West apartment, stared at the phone. It was 2:00 A.M. "I know there was chemistry between us," she said to herself. "He must have been too intimidated by my public image to call." So, feeling very brave, she picked up the phone and called Levine. "I couldn't *believe* I called him," Moore would tell a reporter later. Moore quickly identified herself, then asked Levine, "Do you cook?" "No, I don't," he said. "Neither do I, so I guess we better go out to dinner," Moore decided, and Levine agreed. The following night they dined together.

But Moore, as always, kept her private life a closely guarded secret. When she met with writer Natalie Gittelson while photographers shot pictures of her, first in comfortable jeans, sneakers, and a boy's work shirt and then in more formal wear, Levine's name never came up. Gittelson noted that Moore's face between shots seemed "so haunted by sorrow" that the reporter had to look away. She added, "It must be that the Sunshine Girl of the early '70s has not yet quite fused with the Dark Lady of the early '80s. The effect is heartwrenching." Face to face, though, Moore hid her sadness and chatted eagerly about her new life, her Central Park walks, her workouts with the New York City Ballet, which she managed to arrange because she had friends there. Moore missed the 40-by-60-foot ballet studio in her Bel Air house, but she did enjoy her new life in the Upper West Side of New York, where she had a small apartment and a new circle of friends. Moore spoke of the "feeling of neighborhood" there that was not as formal as the Waldorf Towers had been. She said she preferred the informality of her neighborhood because she is a "white ducks and sneakers person" (despite her status as one of the ten richest women in the country). Moore also spoke of her new film, entitled *Six Weeks*, about a young girl who fulfills her dream of a perfect family by "marrying" her mother (played by Moore) to the father she has always wanted (played by British actor Dudley Moore). Mary called

Dudley Moore (who is not related to her) a "bright sensitive man who listens."

Moore joked with photographers that day, making fun of a new Jane Fonda workout book: "If you get out of bed in the morning, that's a form of exercise. If you bring your fork up to your mouth, that's a form of exercise." However jovial her actions, her words indicated that her sadness still dragged at her like a leaden anchor. She ate hardly any lunch that day, maintaining her strict low-carbohydrate, low-sugar, and low-protein diet that helped to keep her diabetes in check. And she spoke of Tinker:

> Relationships evolve and go through changes. Nothing is forever. . . . We've been conditioned to believe that we can't have a career without a looming male presence to act as guide, mentor and primary decision maker. We've been programmed to accept the idea that without such a male figure at the center of our existence we're really not leading happy and protected lives.

Moore did admit that she would like a man in her life again, but not a husband: "Not somebody who was my strong leader," she said. "Oh, I would like him to be strong, but strong enough to let go." Reflecting on her years since *The Mary Tyler Moore Show*, Moore noted that during all the years she played Mary Richards, she was dealing with themes and dilemmas that she was "just now facing in my own real life: Can I travel with a man whom I don't intend to marry? Should I date simply for dating's sake? Have I got the courage to be alone because I *want* to be alone and for no other reason?" She concluded by saying that "[l]ove, romance and sex are wonderful, of course, but in the end, there's only this that counts: our intrinsic value as individuals."

Moore herself had continued to grow and to insist on her own leadership if there was to be a man in her life again. Although she had dated international millionaire Gordon White and had traveled with him—they stayed in separate hotel rooms—no permanent relationship seemed imminent. In the three years since her divorce from Tinker, Moore had also dated actor and producer Warren Beatty, noted for his performances in the movies *Bonnie and Clyde, Shampoo,* and *Reds*; *Whose Life Is It Anyway?* director Michael Lindsay Hogg; and writer Pete Hamill. In 1983, however, no permanent relationship seemed near. During her photo shoot and interview that day, she coyly admitted to Gittelson that there was a new romance in her life, but she declined to name him.

Within a few months, Levine, 16 years younger than Moore, moved into her apartment, putting an end to her years of trying to learn from Mary Richards just how to play the dating game. "My love for him evolved quickly," Moore told reporter Vernon Scott. "It started as a strong attraction for a wonderful guy, and before I knew it I was a little in love, and then I was a lot in love."

On November 23, 1983, Moore married Levine in a large Jewish ceremony at the Hotel Pierre in New York City. Moore, wearing a simple peach lace antique dress, became Mrs. S. Robert Levine before both of their families and some 300 guests. She was 45, and Levine was 29.

"There's nothing revolutionary in our marriage," Moore told Scott, "but I hope it will encourage women of my age to marry younger men *if that's what they want*." One journalist opened an article on Moore's marriage with "Thank you, Mary, for breaking down another wall."

"The first wall, I suppose, had to do with playing Mary Richards—a single girl without a man in her life," Moore said. "Mary Richards helped so many other women who didn't have dates on Saturday night. Now I guess I've broken down another wall by marrying a younger man."

As Moore continued to model nontraditional lifestyles for American women, Levine helped to change Moore's life for the better. He helped her overcome her shyness and discomfort in crowds, and he persisted when they had disagreements, enabling Moore to get in touch with her feelings. "He's Jewish, and I'm Irish," Moore said. "With my background, when there's an argument, we verbalize it, then walk out and slam the door. There's no way Robert will accept that.

Mary Tyler Moore's only child, Richard Carlton Meeker, Jr. He died from a self-inflicted gunshot wound at age 24.

He takes me by the shoulders and says, 'No. We haven't finished discussing this. Now let's yell! Let's get it out.' That's such a healthy way to settle an argument." Love came more easily for Moore around Levine, too. He helped her become a "toucher and a hugger," she said. And Levine's family came to embrace Moore, which, along with her four years of psychoanalysis, would help her to learn to believe in herself. Most of all, Moore enjoyed being an equal partner with Levine, rather than the daughter that she felt she was with Grant Tinker.

In the summer of 1984 Moore crammed in back-to-back filming of two movies: *Heartsounds*, in Toronto, about Martha Lear, the wife of a doctor dying of heart disease; and

Moore dancing with her fiance, Dr. S. Robert Levine, a cardiologist who had treated her mother. Moore married Levine in 1983.

Finnegan, Begin Again, in Richmond, Virginia, a comedy about a young woman, Liz De Haan, marrying a man in his sixties. That year, a *Working Woman* magazine reviewer told readers, "*Heartsounds*, on ABC-TV, is wonderful . . . don't miss this movie, but have Kleenex handy!" Patricia Bosworth of *Harper's Bazaar* wrote, "*Finnegan, Begin Again* [costarring Robert Preston of *The Music Man* and *Victor, Victoria*, and Sam Waterston of *I'll Fly Away*] would never have been made without the participation of a popular actress like Mary Tyler Moore."

On weekends Levine would fly to the film locations to be with Moore. He even played a small part in *Finnegan, Begin Again* at Moore's urging.

The hectic pace caught up with Moore, however. By fall, her usual pattern of drinking to relax after work or at a dinner or a party was upsetting her body chemistry because of her Type I diabetes. Her three or four shots of insulin per day and her strict diet and exercise regimen could not combat the effects of alcohol, which could cause wildly fluctuating blood sugar levels. Moore's occasional treat of sweet foods and her heavy smoking made matters worse. She would become fatigued and intolerant quickly because of her low blood sugar. As Moore's condition continued to worsen, with more frequent hypoglycemic episodes, she experienced waves of weakness, blurred vision, and slurred speech from low blood sugar levels—all of which could have led to coma or death. In their luxury apartment in New York, Levine studied Moore's blood chemistry, collecting specimens day and night. He suggested she abstain from alcohol until her blood level steadied somewhat.

But Moore was unable to stop on her own. Levine and her doctors suggested that she enter the Betty Ford Center, a chemical dependency recovery hospital in Rancho Mirage, California, to give her a supportive environment in which to stop drinking. In September, Moore was admitted to the center for a six-week stay in a "tough love" program of searingly honest sessions of soul-searching. The program included recognizing alcoholism—whether it took the form of social drinking like Moore's or solitary binging—as a potentially deadly disease.

One of the tenets of programs that help people recover from alcohol or drug addiction is that "the only way out is through"; that is, the only way to be able to stop drinking is to work through, to face, and to manage the reasons for drinking. By taking the first step of admitting herself to the Betty Ford Center, Moore began the crucial process of unburdening herself of so much of her "dark side," her inner anguish, and allowing herself to let go—not to try constantly to be perfect and in control. She gave herself the gift of healing from so much tragedy in her life.

She gave herself the gift of love.

In 1989 Moore, the international chairman of the Juvenile Diabetes Foundation (a non-profit organization), requests funding for research into juvenile diabetes (Type I diabetes) at a House Appropriations Subcommittee meeting on Capitol Hill. Moore is frequently involved in fund-raising efforts for diabetes research.

8

PHOENIX RISING

MARY TYLER MOORE EMERGED from the Betty Ford Center a changed woman. She no longer drank cocktails at the end of the day to relax, and she no longer smoked two and a half packs of cigarettes per day. "And I'm proud of that," she told writer Patricia Nolan. Moore, like anyone addicted to alcohol or drugs, could not have done it on her own. "At the clinic, I met some wonderful people and learned a lot about myself," she said. "I left there a happy and well-balanced person."

Once Moore had given up drinking and smoking she had to deal with the feelings she had been covering up. "I was fearful," she said. "I was uncertain of my own instincts. I've had the kind of fear that I felt stultified my life. It engulfed me," she said. She had also been trying to maintain an image of perfection established by her "nice girl" character, Mary Richards. "I tried very hard to live up to that image 24 hours a day," Moore told Nolan. "I used to push down my inner feelings and desires and ignore my real personal needs—as a way of dealing with others and as a way of hiding the truth from myself, when it became too painful," she said. As part of maintaining an image of perfection, Moore compulsively did things to distract herself from her often painful feelings. She did crossword puzzles and needlepoint constantly. "I thought I was being creative," she said, "but it was another way of not dealing with my real feelings. I hid behind my needlepoint." Moore even felt she was "bad" if she made simple mistakes like dialing a wrong phone number or dropping a towel or a toothpaste cap on the floor. "I was totally unrealistic," she said, "because no one can be perfect at all times, but I tried to be."

Moore gave many interviews to reporters after her rehabilitation at the Betty Ford Center, and when she told them, "I'm not a nice girl anymore," she would explain that she meant she no longer tried to be the perfect Mary Richards, and she no longer felt driven by her compulsions. Most important, she allowed herself to experience her feelings, no matter how powerfully negative they might be. And with her husband, Robert Levine, she was able to express those feelings.

In the year that Moore underwent her rehabilitation, she also devoted herself to a charity especially close to her heart. She committed herself to serving as international chairman of the Juvenile Diabetes Foundation, offering her time, her name, and her money to its fund-raising and research efforts. Over the years, she has become extremely visible in public service campaigns to raise money for diabetes research.

Moore's personal victory did not ensure professional success, however. She returned to weekly television on December 11, 1985, as a divorced fashion writer who gets a consumer advice column at a seamy Chicago tabloid in the CBS sitcom *Mary*. While one critic wrote "Hallelujah, she's back . . . still every woman's idea of a best friend and every man's ideal of womanhood," other critics noted that Moore faced stiff competition from the ghost of her former character, Mary Richards, appearing throughout the country in syn-

In the 1986 film Just Between Friends, *Moore (left) plays a middle-aged housewife and mother of two teenagers whose husband (Ted Danson) dies in a car accident. Moore's character learns that a friend, played by Christine Lahti (right), is pregnant with her recently deceased husband's child.*

dicated reruns of *The Mary Tyler Moore Show*. In *Mary*, Moore's new character, Mary Brenner—worldlier, older, thinner, and more acerbic than Mary Richards, yet surrounded by the same off-the-wall kinds of colleagues—failed to attract the kind of audience that could keep the show afloat. CBS, seeing that *Mary* could not make headway in the Nielsen ratings, canceled it after one season.

Moore next appeared in the movie *Just Between Friends,* written by *The Mary Tyler Moore Show* creator and producer Allan Burns and produced by MTM Enterprises in April 1986. She played a middle-aged homemaker and mother of two teenagers who masters self-reliance and forgiveness after

Moore (left) and Lynn Redgrave (right) play alter egos in the Broadway play Sweet Sue *in 1986. Moore stars as a middle-aged designer of greeting cards who falls in love with her son's roommate (played simultaneously by John Linton and Barry Tubb). The reviewers praised Moore's performance; however, the play itself did not fare as well with the critics.*

her husband, played by Ted Danson (who played Sam Malone in the long-running hit sitcom *Cheers*), dies in a car accident, and she learns that her close friend, a TV newscaster (played by Christine Lahti) will soon bear his child. *New Yorker* film critic Pauline Kael attacked Moore for playing "a role that is tailored for her as she was 15 years ago"—self-conscious and hesitant, adding, "When she flashes that familiar big, bright smile, her face is drawn so taut that she looks as if she's in pain." Yet given the contrast in age and in professional experience between Moore's character and Lahti's confident 29-year-old career woman, and given the shock of discovering the affair after her husband's death, insecurity and pain color Moore's character appropriately.

Moore reversed roles in her next performance, as a middle-aged designer of greeting cards who falls in love with her son's roommate in the play *Sweet Sue.* She and Lynn Redgrave played different versions of the one Sue in each performance, and two male actors played the part of Jake, the target of her (their) affection. Mel Gussow of the *New York Times* wrote that Moore's "comic timing perfected during her years on television suits Susan well . . . [but that the] talented playwright [A. R. Gurney, Jr.] gets less mileage by doubling his cast of characters."

Moore could not understand the critics' dismissals of her recent projects. "It was like drop-kicking a puppy," she told one reporter, revealing her still fragile emotional state.

Finally, on March 27 and 28, 1988, Moore, at age 51, got to play "an actor's dream" role, as she called it: that of Mary Todd Lincoln, wife of President Abraham Lincoln, in *Gore Vidal's Lincoln.* In hoopskirts, Moore whisked her way through the Wickham-Valentine House, a 19th-century mansion in Richmond, Virginia, that served as the White House during filming. Her mastery of an aristocratic Kentucky accent and her controlled portrayal of a woman verging on insanity elicited from her costar Sam Waterston, who played Abraham Lincoln, the breathless praise, "They don't know the half of you." He referred to Moore's faultless rendering of highly emotional scenes in which Mary Todd steals and sells her husband's State of the Union Address, contrives to receive the salary of a former White House employee so she can pay off bills from her compulsive shopping sprees, and refuses to let her youngest son, Thomas, join the army because two of his older brothers have already died.

Moore did not at all resemble the former first lady, who was short, plump, and plain, but this did not deter her. "It's the essence I'm portraying, not the demeanor," she told reporter Doug Hill. Moore's concern that the script did not sufficiently explore the sources of Mary Todd Lincoln's bizarre behavior prompted director Lamont Johnson to call for script revisions. She worried too that her Mary Richards character would remain uppermost in the minds of viewers, draining her Mary Todd Lincoln of credibility. Thinking it over, she concluded, "I'm going to have to give the public credit for being a little more mature than that—and a little more able to lose themselves in a story." Moore worked hard to ensure that she refrained from using her "bag of tricks"—gestures, inflections, and expressions that she had perfected over the years as her trademarks—that were inappropriate to a woman of the Victorian era. Her diligence and her attention to detail paid off because "everyone on location [was] impressed with the acting of Mary Tyler Moore," Hill wrote. Critic John Leonard could not keep his mind on Waterston's Lincoln for Moore's Mary Todd—her "jealous rages, incapacitating migraine headaches." Reenacting the tragedy of Mary Todd's losing her husband and three of her four children (she was declared insane 10 years after Lincoln's death), "Moore brought uneasiness and fragility, holding herself by the elbows as if afraid she'd drop and shatter," Leonard wrote. Perhaps aware of Moore's concerns about her believability in the role, Leonard begrudgingly acknowledged the undeniable evolution of Moore's professional persona and confessed his own Mary Tyler Moore hang-up. He wrote,

> I wanted to ride to her rescue. Couldn't she be Dolly Madison instead? We grew up with Mary at work and Mary in love and Mary in our living rooms. In my heart, she's always tossing her hat in the air, preserved in a kind of electronic aspic, even in reruns at three in the morning, when it seems I need her most; and there I was, caring more about her than I did about the Civil War. Mary shouldn't suffer. History, bloody history, ought not to have happened to her. Well. So she's forever our child in this peculiar and demanding and intimate blue living room light, with the happy ending and we *own her?* It's a scary, shameful sort of smother love.

Moore's Mary Todd was a success. She won an Emmy Award for the performance. But affection and nostalgia for Mary Richards would still have her eliciting thoughts of her

Moore portrays the emotionally unstable Mary Todd Lincoln and Sam Waterston stars as her husband, Abraham, in Gore Vidal's Lincoln, *a television miniseries broadcast in March 1988. Moore's acting won her an Emmy Award and raves from the critics.*

WJM-TV persona in the minds and hearts of the viewers of *Gore Vidal's Lincoln.*

It seemed that Moore herself could not get away from the memory and the dream of starring in a television sitcom. On October 26, 1988, CBS launched *Annie McGuire*, in which she played a divorcée who remarries a divorced blue-collar dad and inherits his two children. Executive producer Elliott Schoeman said, "Annie's a lot like Mary herself. They've both been through a lot; they are women of maturity and control." But, as with *Mary*, this series failed to find its market, and the network canceled it. The last show aired on December 28, 1988.

Moore's career may have been on-again, off-again, skipping beats, out of tune with the times, or just not designed well enough for Moore, but at home she and her husband continued to be happy together. They divided their time between their 14-room apartment in Manhattan overlooking Central Park, and their 29-acre estate, "Greenlawn," in Millbrook in upstate New York. With the sale of MTM Enterprises to a British broadcasting company in 1988, Moore had netted $113 million in cash and stock, so she did not need to earn an income.

Moore opened up both residences to *Architectural Digest* photographers in 1991 and shared with the public her thoughts about creating her and her husband's unique living spaces. Their Manhattan apartment could pass for an elegant museum, housing floor-to-ceiling modern paintings, clay figures dating from before Columbus landed in the Americas, and Chinese and English antiques. Paintings of deep red hearts flank the living room fireplace, and Moore's leather-bound scripts from her TV series and movies are shelved in the library. The overall effect reflects Moore's self-proclaimed California persona—an affinity for light-filled spaces and a dislike for what she calls a "cozy dark atmosphere."

Moore and Levine decided to move from their previous cooperative apartment in Central Park West when the area changed from a peaceful blend of ethnic neighborhoods to a conflux of T-shirt stores and raucous Saturday night crowds. The old neighborhood had "lost its charm" for Moore, so, she said, "I decided it was time to leave my carefree bohemian days and move over to the East Side to join the grown-ups."

One glimpse of her Manhattan apartment would quell forever the myriad speculations about Mary Tyler Moore and Mary Richards being one and the same. Writer Meryl Gordon contrasted the sophistication of the New York apartment to the homespun 1970s simplicity of Mary Richards's television apartment, with its shag rugs, exposed brick wall, wicker coffee table, and large gold *M* on the wall. Moore held on to the *M* over the years but finally gave it away to a charity fundraiser. In his usual thoughtful manner, Levine bought it back for her, and now it hangs discretely on a home office wall. In Moore's apartment it is surrounded by priceless art, including a bronze horse by the French painter and sculptor Henri Matisse and a sketch by the Russian artist Marc Chagall.

Moore is not all complex sophistication, though. She designed her New York apartment in contrast to the way she and Levine live in the country, "which is [in] baggy jeans and dirty sneakers," she told Gordon. Greenlawn's compound includes a renovated stucco, stone, and clapboard Tudor hunting cabin and additions such as a dance studio for Moore. Waterfalls connect the seven ponds on the property, and stables house the couple's horses. Most significantly, the home's interior affords Moore an opportunity to dabble in one of her favorite pastimes, hunting for antiques and American folk art. "Up here I'm notorious—I love to prowl the stores looking for . . . stuff that stands out and speaks to me," she said. Greenlawn also includes a garden, giving Moore "the chance to entertain in a relaxed way, the chance to do things that I had not trained myself to do—like fiddle with flowers, to finally know the difference between an annual and a perennial; to be able to go into the vegetable garden and fool around a little bit," Moore told writer Steven Aronson. Moore spoke of her mare, Fanny, who was going to foal soon. "She's going to put her babe on the ground, as they say," Moore said. "To

On September 8, 1992, Moore reacts to the press and her fans after being honored with a star on Hollywood's renowned Walk of Fame.

be a part of *that!*" Moore enjoys the reward of seeing the results of short-term projects. A weekly TV series, she said, was "abstract . . . you do it and you don't see it for about six weeks, and then you see it and it's gone. . . . You never really see the fruits of your labor, I think, in the kind of business I'm in. But having a place like this changes all that—three falls ago I planted 325 daffodil bulbs, and that spring I saw 325 of those suckers come up."

Moore and Levine sat on the front lawn and posed for photographer Durston Saylor. Moore, with short honey-colored hair, bangs brushed across her forehead, sat cross-legged, leaning back toward Levine as dappled sunlight played across their smiling faces. Moore loosely held the reins of Fanny, and Levine held those of his chestnut horse.

Inside, Moore led the photographer and writer through her raspberry-colored octagonal entranceway, where stately portraits of Moore's ancestors Colonel Lewis Tilghman Moore and John C. Schindler hang on the walls. A portrait of old, white-bearded Captain John Moore, painted in the 19th century by Elizabeth Moore Reid, hangs in the wood-paneled library, where Moore keeps her Lincoln collection, "all the stuff I collected in preparation for . . . *Gore Vidal's Lincoln,*" she said. There too is Moore's Emmy Award for that performance, along with the four other Emmys she had won, the three Golden Globe Awards, the Academy Award nomination, and the honorary Tony Award.

Moore's sense of American history and of her roots shows itself most clearly in an eagle-patterned hooked rug hung above the living room fireplace. Evidence of the love that she and Levine share appears on the dining room wall in the *ketubah,* the Hebrew word meaning "marriage contract." Their ketubah is written on what looks like tablets of stone, framed by illustrations of various symbols of their lives together: a mountain for Mt. Sinai Hospital (where they met), theatrical masks for Moore's acting, and so on.

Moore went upstairs to the second floor, passing a red, white, and blue Amish quilt and a raspberry-colored powder room, with antique game boards on the walls. She noted in passing that all the furniture in both her homes is dog proof because Dudley, her French hunting dog ("No, he's not named after Dudley Moore," she added, laughing), and Dash, her golden retriever, are allowed on every piece. The dogs have their own hot and cold showers so Moore can keep them clean. (The animal-loving Moore was elected to the board of the American Society for the Prevention of Cruelty to Animals [ASPCA].)

At the foot of the stairs Moore pointed out a collection of miniature chairs hanging on the wall, then headed out to the kitchen with its oversized stone hearth. Outside on the grounds eucalyptus, willow, poplar, black walnut, and evergreen trees offer repose. *"I talk* to these trees," Moore said. "Do they talk back? Yes they do. It has a very calming effect. Very calming." Moore walked to her swimming pool, where she swims laps to work out; it is rebuilt in a turquoise and green checkerboard pattern "to give it a little sparkle."

Moore and Levine found Greenlawn in 1987 after having searched for a home for four years. They began by looking at city apartments with terraces, but they could not find the right mix of space and neighborhood. The longer they looked, the farther they got from the city. "[We] lived like gypsies," she said, moving from the main house to the caretaker's cottage and sleeping on cots until renovations on the house were finished. Moore said of her 18th house, "You can't do anything that looks as relaxed and informal as this without a lot of organization, you know," adding, "that's it— this is it, this is my sign off."

Moore had not signed off from her career, however. On November 4, 1990, ABC aired *The Last Best Year,* a television movie pairing Moore as psychologist Wendy Allen and Bernadette Peters as Jane Murray, a dying patient. Allen is reluctant at first to take Murray as a patient because as a child she was shut out of her own father's death from cancer, and she has not resolved her anger over it. The two become friends, though, and Allen reveals to her mother and to her therapist her anger and her fear of Jane's death. "Neither has ever been better at doing what they do best, which is to make you love them as much as we would want to be loved ourselves," John Leonard wrote in *New York* magazine. A self-proclaimed cynic, Leonard confessed to having "a tear in the eye and a lump in the throat" while watching the film. He repeated his reluctance to accept Moore as anything other than a happy young woman "throwing her hat in the air," saying, "Moore adds another anguished glaze to the very different picture we got of her in *Ordinary People* and as Mary Todd Lincoln," concluding that her "terrific smile" that "used to be a gift must now be earned."

In October 1991, Moore opened the TV special "Funny Women of Television," which was designed to show "who broke ground where," according to its executive producer Jack Haley, Jr. (he cited *The Mary Tyler Moore Show* as one of the top "breakthrough shows"). "Despite the light-years she'd advanced the cause of women, Mary still felt it necessary to define herself in . . . nurturant, maternal terms," claimed a *Savvy* magazine writer in 1988. "And TV heroines today define themselves . . . with Mary."

In March 1993, Moore portrayed an elderly woman, Georgia Tann, who sold babies on the black market, in the television movie *Stolen Babies*. A *New York* magazine critic called the movie an "intelligent and provocative film," in which "we are asked to root against Mary Tyler Moore." Moore won her seventh Emmy Award for this role. The first words of her acceptance speech at the awards ceremony were "Sorry, Ed," to Ed Asner, because her win meant that they were tied for the greatest number of prime-time Emmy Awards won by a performer.

Moore joined the growing number of female celebrities making exercise videos in 1994 with *Mary Tyler Moore: Aerobics* and *Mary Tyler Moore: Body Sculpting*, both part of the Everywoman's Workout series. On October 29 of that year she joined the ranks of leading comedians when she was honored at "The Second Annual Comedy Hall of Fame Television Show." Dick Van Dyke, narrating an overview of her life, called her "bright, charming, uplifting, generous and nice? . . . *Never.* . . . She's *the nicest.*" In accepting the award, Moore said, "I've been blessed with an abundance of creative individuals around me." She named Carl Reiner, Allan Burns,

and Jim Brooks, and finally, she jokingly—and then serious-
ly—thanked Grant Tinker "for giving up a career as a tennis
bum" to guide her career through "the shark-infested waters"
of show business.

In January 1995, *Entertainment Tonight* reporters found
Moore on the set of a new movie, *Keys to Tulsa,* her first feature film in a decade, which costarred James Spader, James
Coburn, and Eric Stolz and was released later that year. She
responded candidly to the reporters' assumptions that she did
not do more films because there was a dearth of interesting
roles. "It's not so much that I've been selective, as the big
screen has been selective," she said. "So I don't do this as
often as I'd like to." She said that she was still doing "the
things that aging actresses are supposed to do," such as gar-
dening, and she added with a smile, "I'm experimenting with
life as it was meant to be led."

However, Moore has found some roles that are to her lik-
ing. She filmed *The Rose Garden,* a drama for the Family
Channel that aired in late 1995. In early 1996, Moore portrayed another character that is in sharp contrast to her usual
wide-eyed, innocent type, in *Flirting with Disaster,* a film
with George Segal, Ben Stiller, and Patricia Arquette.

Around that time she also starred in a television drama
about a no-nonsense editor of a fictional tabloid, *New York
News*—continuing to build her characterization as a tough
1990s woman. "It doesn't interest me anymore to play a . . .
very nice, very likeable, somewhat naive, vulnerable character—all those adorable features of the two ladies [Laura
Petrie and Mary Richards] that I played," she said. In evolv-
ing through those television roles Moore represented the shift
in identities of women throughout the second half of the 20th
century: from homemaker to working single woman, "grentioning" and "fumphering" her way through a predominately
male world, to boss—a woman on her own and in charge.

Life, Moore had come to learn, was meant to be led from
the heart—openly, honestly, and *not* perfectly—not just from
discipline and an iron will. Only by understanding this could

Moore prepares to make an awards announcement at a ceremony in 1992. In the fall of 1995, after more than 35 years in television, Moore returned to CBS with a dramatic role as the tough editor-in-chief of a tabloid called New York News.

she survive, flourish, and prosper. For Moore, success had come to mean not awards on a shelf or Nielsen ratings or movie roles but the deep, abiding peace of coming to terms with herself.

Moore told *Redbook*'s Kathy Henderson in 1988 that she no longer blamed God for the tragedies in her life. There "is no answer," she said. "In living through the worst, you become acutely aware of how easily the worst can happen—when you least expect it—and there's nothing you can do about it." She added, "I think my experiences have made me fatalistic in a good sense. I don't ask God, 'Why me?' anymore. I'm all right now. I can look back at the happy times, but I can also look back at the *unhappy ones* and say 'That's all right.' . . . I'm happier now than I've ever been."

Like the phoenix, the mythical bird that rose from its own ashes, Moore gave the world her sweetness as Mary Richards, then, surviving tragedy, remade herself into the stately and sophisticated actress whose smile, as John Leonard wrote, "would have to be earned by the world." For Mary Tyler Moore, love was no longer just "all around." It was inside.

FURTHER READING

Alley, Robert S., and Irby B. Brown. *Love Is All Around: The Making of the Mary Tyler Moore Show*. New York: Delacourte, 1989.

Aronson, Steven M. L. "Architectural Digest Visits Mary Tyler Moore: A Complete Retreat for the Actress and Her Husband in Upstate New York." *Architectural Digest*, 48 (June 1991): 118–27.

Balley, Diane. "Mary Richards Would Be Married Today." *TV Guide*, 39 (October 19–25, 1991): 13.

Birmingham, Frederic A. "30 a Week and Lots of Credit Cards." *Saturday Evening Post*, 246 (October 1974): 74–77.

Boodro, M. "Finnegan, Begin Again." *Harpers Bazaar*, 118 (February 1985): 57.

Bosworth, Patricia. "Laugh, Cry, Be Thoroughly Entertained." *Working Woman*, 9 (October 1984): 168.

Bowers, John. "From TV to Tiffany's in One Wild Leap." *Saturday Evening Post*, 239 (November 1966): 97–101.

Davidson, Muriel. "Bright New World of Mary Tyler Moore." *Good Housekeeping*, 171 (January 1971): 59.

The Dick Van Dyke Show. Nick at Night TV. 1994. Videocassette.

Gittelson, Natalie. "Mary Tyler Moore Is in Good Shape." *McCalls*, 110 (January 1983): 76–77.

Gordon, Meryl. "Mary Tyler Moore's Manhattan." *Architectural Digest*, 48 (December 1991): 126–33.

Greenfield, Jeffrey. *Television, the First Fifty Years*. New Orleans: Crescent Books, 1981.

Gussow, Mel. "Holly Go Quickly." *Newsweek*, 68 (December 26, 1966): 45.

Harrison, Barbara Grizzuti. "I'm Not a Nice Girl Anymore." *McCalls*, 113 (January 1986): 70–71.

Henderson, Kathy. "Mary Tyler Moore: 'I'm All Right Now.' " *Redbook*, 171 (May 1988): 20.

Hill, Doug. "Playing a Woman Who Stole and Sold Her Husband's State of the Union Address." *TV Guide*, 36 (March 26–April 1, 1988): 8–9.

"How To Succeed Though Married." *Time*, 85 (April 9, 1965): 62.

Jarvis, Jeff. "Picks and Pans." *People's Weekly*, 24 (December 16, 1985): 15.

Johnston, Tracey. "Why 30 Million Are Mad About Mary." *New York Times Magazine*, April 7, 1974, 30.

Kael, Pauline. "Just Between Friends." *The New Yorker*, 62 (May 5, 1986): 118–19.

Kroll, Jack. *Newsweek*, 95 (March 10, 1980): 103.

Kulzer, Dina Marie. *Television Series Regulars of the Fifties and Sixties in Interview*. Jefferson, NC: McFarland, 1992.

Lague, Louise A. "Potentially Deadly Dependence on Alcohol Sends Mary Tyler Moore to the Betty Ford Center." *People's Weekly*, 22 (October 1, 1984): 38–42.

Leonard, John. "Gore Vidal's Lincoln." *New York*, 21 (April 25, 1988): 122.

———. "The Last Best Year." *New York*, 23 (November 5, 1990): 113.

The Mary Tyler Moore Show. Nick at Night TV. 1994. Videocassette.

Maynard, Joyce. "Is Mary Tyler Moore Too Good to Be True?" *McCalls*, 101 (March 1974): 28.

Moore, Mary Tyler. "Living My Life My Way." *New Choices for the Best Years*, 28 (December 1988): 18.

O'Connor, Thomas. "Mary Tyler Moore." *New York Times Biographical Service*, 16 (December 1985): 1461–62.

Polskin, Howard. "Two Lighthearted Actresses Tackle a Heavyweight Drama." *TV Guide*, 38 (November 3–9, 1990): 27–29.

Rovin, Jeff. "The Special Strength of Mary Tyler Moore." *Ladies Home Journal,* 102 (April 1985): 104–5.

Rudolph, Ileane. "Mary Tyler Moore." *TV Guide*, 41 (March 13–19, 1993): 10–12.

Scott, Vernon. "Four Fascinating Women." *Ladies Home Journal*, 92 (September 1975): 86.

Stewart-Gordon, James. "Everyone's Mad About Mary." *Readers Digest*, 105 (October 1974): 25–28.

Tinker, Grant. *Tinker in Television*. New York: Simon & Schuster, 1994.

Waters, H. F. "Mary." *Newsweek*, 106 (December 9, 1985): 60–62.

Winship, Michael. *Television*. New York: Random House, 1988.

Wooley, Lynn M., et al. *Warner Brothers Television: Major Shows of the Fifties and Sixties Episode-by-Episode*. Jefferson, NC: McFarland, 1985.

CHRONOLOGY

1937   Born Mary Moore on December 29 in Brooklyn, New York

1944   Takes ballet lessons

1946   Moves with her family to Los Angeles, California

1955   Lands her first acting job as the Happy Hotpoint elf, earning $5,000 for a series of TV ads; marries Richard Meeker

1956   Gives birth to son, Richard Carlton Meeker, Jr., in July

1957–59   Works as a chorus-line dancer on *The Eddie Fisher Show* and *The George Gobel Show*; lands her first speaking role in *The Burns and Allen Show*; appears on *The Bob Cummings Show* and *Bachelor Father*; wins the part of Sam, the sultry receptionist, on *Richard Diamond, Private Detective*

1960   Wins the part of Laura Petrie in the television comedy series *The Dick Van Dyke Show*

1961   Plays Pamela Stewart in her first movie, *X-15*

1962   Divorces Meeker

1963   Marries Grant Tinker on June 1

1964   Wins Emmy Award for Outstanding Continued Performance by an Actress in a Leading Role in a Comedy Series; miscarries her pregnancy and learns she has Type I diabetes

1965   Wins Foreign Press Golden Globe Award for Best Female Television Personality of the Year

1966   Awarded Emmy for Outstanding Continued Performance by an Actress in a Leading Role in a Comedy Series; tapes her last segment as Laura Petrie on March 22; plays prostitute Holly Golightly in the Broadway musical *Breakfast at Tiffany's*

1967   Costars with Julie Andrews in *Thoroughly Modern Millie*

1969   Offered her own television series by all three networks; founds MTM Enterprises with Tinker

1970   *The Mary Tyler Moore Show*, in which Moore plays Mary Richards, airs for the first time on CBS on September 19

1973   Awarded the Emmy for Outstanding Continued Performance by an Actress in a Leading Role in a Comedy Series; in November, Moore and Tinker separate

1974	Moore and Tinker reconcile after six weeks; Moore receives two Emmys: Best Actress in a Comedy Series and Actress of the Year–Series
1977	The last episode of *The Mary Tyler Moore Show* airs on March 19
1978	Moore's sister, Elizabeth, commits suicide; Moore receives an Emmy nomination for Best Actress in a Special for *First, You Cry*
1979	Moore and Tinker separate
1980	Moore's son, Richie, dies of a self-inflicted gunshot wound; Moore wins a Tony Award for *Whose Life Is It Anyway?*
1981	Wins Golden Globe Award and is nominated for Academy Award for Best Actress for her performance in *Ordinary People;* Moore and Tinker divorce
1983	Costars with Dudley Moore in *Six Weeks*; marries cardiologist Dr. S. Robert Levine on November 23
1984	Receives an Emmy Award nomination for the television movie *Heartsounds;* appears in *Finnegan, Begin Again;* enters Betty Ford Center in September for six weeks of treatment to stop drinking alcohol
1985	Stars in sitcom *Mary*; inducted into Television Hall of Fame
1986	Costars with Ted Danson in the television movie *Just Between Friends*
1988	Plays Mary Todd Lincoln in TV miniseries *Gore Vidal's Lincoln* and wins an Emmy Award for her performance; launches new sitcom *Annie McGuire*; sells MTM Enterprises to a British company
1990	Costars with Bernadette Peters in *The Last Best Year*
1994	Makes two exercise videos; is inducted into the Comedy Hall of Fame on October 29
1995	Plays matriarch of a southern family in movie *Keys to Tulsa;* appears in the drama *The Rose Garden* on the Family Channel; stars in *Flirting with Disaster;* plays the tough editor-in-chief of the tabloid *New York News* in a drama aired by the CBS network in the fall

INDEX

Margaret L. Finn, a native of Philadelphia, Pennsylvania, holds a B.A. in sociology from the University of Pennsylvania and an M.A. in English from Beaver College, where she also taught freshman composition. She has produced an alumni magazine for the Wharton Graduate School of Business of the University of Pennsylvania, and she is fiction editor of the literary journal *Northeast Corridor*.

Jerry Lewis is the National chairman of the Muscular Dystrophy Association (MDA) and host of the MDA Labor Day Telethon. An internationally acclaimed comedian, Lewis began his entertainment career in New York and then performed in a comedy team with singer and actor Dean Martin from 1946 to 1956. Lewis has appeared in many films—including *The Delicate Delinquent, Rock a Bye Baby, The Bellboy, Cinderfella, The Nutty Professor, The Disorderly Orderly,* and *The King of Comedy*—and his comedy performances, such as his 1995 role in the Broadway play *Damn Yankees*, continue to delight audiences around the world.

John Callahan is a nationally syndicated cartoonist and the author of an illustrated autobiography, *Don't Worry, He Won't Get Far on Foot*. He has also produced three cartoon collections: *Do Not Disturb Any Further, Digesting the Child Within, and Do What He Says! He's Crazy!!!* He has recently been the subject of feature articles in the *New York Times Magazine*, the *Los Angeles Times Magazine*, and the Cleveland Plain Dealer, and has been profiled on *60 Minutes*. Callahan resides in Portland, Oregon.

PICTURE CREDITS

Every effort has been made to contact the copyright owners of photographs and illustrations used in this book. In the event that the holder of a copyright has not heard from us, he or she should contact Chelsea House Publishers.

AP/Wide World Photos: pp. 12, 44, 55, 75, 90, 101, 102, 111, 114; Archive Photos: pp. 28 (photo by Curt Gunther), 49, 72, (photo by Ron Galella); The Bettmann Archive: pp. 23, 56; Photofest: pp. 27, 33, 34, 38, 40, 60, 63, 64, 68, 76, 81, 88, 95, 96, 107, 108, 119; St. Rose of Lima School: p. 24; UPI/Bettmann Archive: pp. 15, 16, 20, 30, 37, 67, 84, 104; UPI/Bettmann Newsphotos: pp. 2 (frontispiece), 50.